ED YOUNG

SEXUAL REVOLUTION

GOD CREATED IT.
CULTURE REDEFINED IT.
WHO GOT IT RIGHT?

STUDY GUIDE

Copyright © 2007 by Edwin B. Young. All rights reserved.

Written permission must be secured from the author to use or reproduce any part of this book, except for occasional page copying for personal study or brief quotations in critical reviews or articles.

Ed Young Resources
Published in Dallas, TX by Creality Publishing.

All Scripture quotations, unless otherwise noted, are taken from The Holy Bible, New International Version (North American Edition), copyright © 1973, 1978, 1984 by the International Bible Society. Used by permission of Zondervan Publishing House.

Any emphases or parenthetical comments within Scripture are the author's own.

ISBN 10: 1-934146-39-0
ISBN 13: 978-1-934146-39-2

Cover Design and Layout: Jason Acker Design

CONTENTS

Week 1	Stripped	7
	Devotionals	18
Week 2	Heaven on Earth	29
	Devotionals	40
Week 3	Leashed	51
	Devotionals	62
Week 4	Do Your Thing	73
	Devotionals	84
Week 5	Messed Up	95
	Devotionals	106

LEADER'S GUIDE

Week 1	Stripped	117
Week 2	Heaven on Earth	123
Week 3	Leashed	129
Week 4	Do Your Thing	135
Week 5	Messed Up	141

HOW TO USE THIS BOOK

Small Groups are a vital part of how we do ministry at Fellowship Church, just as they are in many churches around the world. There are a number of different theories on how small groups should work and they are all great in different ways. The book you are holding is written with our model in mind. So take a minute to read the following explanation, then feel free to adapt as necessary.

Each of our small groups practices a three part agenda in every meeting. That agenda includes a social time, a discussion time, and a prayer time. Each of these elements share equal importance, but not necessarily equal time. To help you get the most out of this book we have included an explanation of each of the parts.

The first element of every small group meeting should be a time of socializing. This phase of the meeting should be about 30% of your time together. Welcome everyone as they arrive at the host home, and make visitors feel welcome by introducing yourself and the other members of your small group. Enjoy some snacks, or if your group prefers, a meal together.

Then move on with second part of the meeting, the lesson. The lesson itself may take as much as 50% of your group's meeting time, but remember, it is not the most important element. You may want to start this phase of your meeting with a short "icebreaker" to get everyone talking. The questions in the "Start it Up" section of each chapter are what we refer to as "level the playing field" questions that everyone should be able to participate in, regardless of their level of spiritual maturity or Bible knowledge. As your group moves through the "Talk it Up" section in each chapter, remember that it is more important to finish on time than to finish each and every question. It is okay to skip some questions to be sure you allow enough time to take care of the third phase of the small group time: "Lift it Up."

The "Lift it Up" section is a vital part of every small group meeting and should be about 20% of the meeting. During this time you will be able to share with the group what God is doing in your life as well as asking the group to support you in specific prayers. To help focus this time, there are one or two questions at the end of each study that will prompt prayers based on the material you have just talked about. There is also a space for you to write down your prayer request(s) so you don't forget them and so you can communicate them clearly when it is your turn. Below that is a place to write down the prayer requests of the people in your group so you can remember and pray for each request throughout the week.

As an additional tool to assist you in your journey of spiritual development, there is a "Step it Up" section at the end of each session. This section consists of five devotional thoughts that reinforce the lesson you've just completed and are designed to help you develop a regular quiet time with God. To get the absolute most from this study, I challenge you to take five or ten minutes a day to read and apply these devotionals to your life. If your group meets twice a month or bi-weekly, choose five of the intervening days to incorporate these thoughts into your devotional life.

In select studies, we have incorporated special notes for youth groups using this material. You will notice a special icon (Y) used several times in each session. This indicates that there is a comment or question especially for youth included in the leader's guide for that part of the study. When you see that icon, simply turn to the leader's guide for that session in the back of the book and find the corresponding (Y) and letter (for instance, (Y)-a). These notes are designed to help each discussion time connect with the unique needs and issues of youth.

SEXUAL REVOLUTION

Do you realize that the first question asked about you was a sexual one? Really, before you even entered the world, people were already associating you with sex. 'Is it a boy or is it a girl?'

Everyone is sexual; God made us that way. He made some of us to be male and some of us female. But most importantly, God made us to be human. God's goal for us is to be fully human – fully alive!

What does it mean to be fully human? It means that we have physical bodies and spiritual bodies. An animal is just a physical body, and angels are just spiritual, but God brought those two beings together when he created man and woman in his image.

Because we are fully physical and fully spiritual, everything we do impacts our body, mind and spirit. That means sex is spiritual! If we want to live the life God wants for us, we must understand both the physical and spiritual dynamics of sex.

In this study we are going to reconnect God with sex. We will take a look at the awesome choices we have related to our sexuality and how to revolutionize our lives and relationships by moving closer to God's incredible design for sex.

Let the Revolution Begin!

WEEK ONE

STRIPPED

SEXUAL REVOLUTION

START IT UP

Some of us lived through it. Others of us are here as a result of it. And still others may have no idea what it was. I'm talking about the cultural phenomenon of the 1960s—the sexual revolution.

1. Of all the changes in our world since the 1960s, which ones do you think have been the best and worst?

_____
_____
_____
_____

One definition of revolution is "change that ushers in something better." The sexual revolution of the 1960s brought change; but did it bring positive change? Or could it be that we've been lied to? Could it be that the revolution was really a grand scale illusion that only brought about widespread pollution?

STRIPPED SEXUAL REVOLUTION

This study is designed to start another sexual revolution—not one like the 1960s version, but one that has the power and the grace of God to bring about a sudden change for our best. Over the next several weeks, we're going to look at sex through the eyes of God and see the potential it has to revolutionize our lives. But change always brings about some conflict. And oftentimes, people get nervous when they think of sex and God in the same arena.

If the thought of talking about sex within the context of God and the Bible makes you tense, you are not thinking right. I read a while back that the average man has a sexual thought every twenty seconds. I would venture to say that women think about it often as well. So the issue is not that we don't think about sex. The problem is, we don't think deeply enough about it. Over the next several weeks (and hopefully for the rest of your life) we're going to take off the floaties and dive deep as we discover what it means to do sex God's way.

To revolutionize our view of sex, we've got to first learn to think right. For too long, people have separated sex and God. In effect, we've kicked the bed out of church and the church out of bed. We're going to bring the bed back in church and the church back in bed. And we're going to ultimately recognize something revolutionary—sex is worship.

TALK IT UP

What comes to your mind when you think about a bed? For some of you, it's a place of beauty, relaxation, comfort. You picture a bed with a comforter, decorative pillows, and nice 800 thread count sheets. For you, the bed is a refuge, a place to rest and recharge. The bed is a symbol of intimacy where you and your spouse have sexual intercourse—where you make love. (Y)-a

For others, the bed is a place to crash, to sack out. The sheets are rarely even laundered and the bed in never made. It's chaotic. It is not a place of intimacy, but a place of rebellion. It could be that the bed is a place of regret for you because you've been sleeping in the wrong bed with the wrong person.

Or maybe you're single and wondering, "Will someone ever occupy the other side of the bed? Will I ever get married?"

However you view it, the bed is a powerful symbol that can bring a variety of images and questions to our minds. But of all the images, church is probably not one of them. And thinking of the bed in church is strange and uncomfortable for us because most of us were never taught to think right about sex within the context of God's design.

2. Growing up, what did you learn about sex—either from your parents or your church? ⓨ-b

_____

_____

_____

_____

Most of us did not grow up in a church where we heard the right teaching about sex. I doubt very many of us grew up in an environment where sex was talked about lovingly and openly. The result is that some people have the idea that we should just suppress our sexuality. And for far too long, the church has said simply one thing about our sexuality, "You're not really a sexual being. Just deny those desires. When they begin to surface, just take a cold shower."

Others have been taught by culture to overly express their sexuality and go for it with whomever, whenever, and however. Their mantra is, "Just do it!" For them, it's all about the buzz and the high and the thrill and the chill of having sex anywhere, anytime and with anyone. If that is your mindset, you, too, are missing something essential about sex.

When it comes to our sexuality, the church has taught us one thing: not to. Culture, on the other hand has only taught us how to. This revolution is going to teach us when to, why to, and who to so that we can get the most out of our sexuality.

Sex is a God-given gift. But so often, it is used in a God-forbidden way. We've got to take this God-given gift and use it in a God-driven way. Sex is a supernatural gift reserved for a man and a woman in the context of marriage. What is marriage? It's a covenant between a man and a woman; a lifelong commitment that is to be supported, protected and fought for—no matter what.

3. Why do you think God designed sex for the context of the marriage and not as a gift to be shared flippantly? ⓨ-c

_____

_____

_____

_____

When it comes to the revolution, right thinking is paramount. But here is something else we may never have considered: Sex is something we are before it's something that we do. All of us are sexual. If you're a single adult, you're sexual. If you're a teenager, you're sexual. If you're a married with three kids and two dogs and a mortgage, you're sexual. Everyone's sexual. God intentionally made us that way, so it's something we are before it's something that we do.

BEING FULLY HUMAN

The beginning of the Bible tells us that the earth was formless and void. It was chaotic. And in Genesis 1:2, the Bible says, "...the Spirit of the Lord was hovering over the waters." That word "hovering" is the word picture of a bird hovering over her nest to protect and provide for her young. It was in this context that God began his creative process. As he did, the creations became more complex as the days went on. On day five, God created his most complex creation to that point.

> And God said, "Let the land produce living creatures according to their kinds: livestock, creatures that move along the ground, and wild animals, each according to its kind." And it was so. God made the wild animals according to their kinds, the livestock according to their kinds, and all the creatures that move along the ground according to their kinds. And God saw that it was good. Genesis 1:24-25

Notice what God is doing. He is creating the animals. But you're not an animal. God had not finished his creative process yet. There was one more

SEXUAL REVOLUTION STRIPPED

creation to be made—human beings. Humans are not animals. I know for some that might be revolutionary, but you are not animals.

Throughout Genesis chapter one, we see a distinct rhythm in the description of God's creative process. But in Genesis 1:26, the rhythm breaks abruptly. The original writer intentionally broke the rhythm in order to show the uniqueness of what it means to be a man or a woman.

> Then God said, "Let us make man in our image, in our likeness, and let them rule over the fish of the sea and the birds of the air, over the livestock, over all the earth, and over all the creatures that move along the ground."
>
> So God created man in his own image, in the image of God he created him; male and female he created them. Genesis 1:26-27

4. What do you think it means to be made in the image of God? Ⓨ-d

_____

_____

_____

_____

Being made in the image of God means we are both physical and spiritual. We have a physical body and a spiritual soul. There's integration with the physical and the spiritual. And because of that, there is no such thing as a separate spiritual life. The physical and the spiritual are inseparable.

Being made in the image of God also means we're made uniquely male and uniquely female. There is a unique masculine soul and there is a unique feminine soul. Thus, when a husband and wife have sexual intercourse in the marriage bed, they are reflecting the full nature and the character of God. You've got the masculine character qualities and the feminine character qualities uniting in the most physical and most spiritual act of worship.

When we have sex outside of God's design, though, we're having what I call "little sex." Little sex is not what God had in mind when he created us. It leads

STRIPPED SEXUAL REVOLUTION

to nothing but trouble. God wants us to have big sex—sex that will lead us to a great life. (Y)-e

Sex is significant, but many people are having little sex. If you buy into the culture's idea that it is "just sex," then you are having little sex. You are missing the physical and spiritual side of sex. If we want to have big sex; if we hope to start this sexual revolution, we must first recognize that we're made in the image of God, who wants the best for all of our lives.

> *The LORD God said, "It is not good for the man to be alone. I will make a helper suitable for him."* Genesis 2:18

After each piece of creation God looked at what he had done and said, "It is good." However, after God looked at the man he created, he said, "It is not good for man to be alone." God was not satisfied with man going through his existence on earth alone. What did God do? Did he leave man on his own? No. God decided to create a suitable helper for Adam—Eve.

> *Then the LORD God made a woman from the rib he had taken out of the man, and he brought her to the man.* Genesis 2:22

Scripture does not tell us what went on when Adam first saw Eve, but try to imagine Adam's surprise. Here's Adam, who has been alone until God makes a perfect woman for him, and all of a sudden God presents this woman to him as a perfect companion—emotionally, spiritually, and even physically!

> *The man said, "This is now bone of my bones and flesh of my flesh; she shall be called 'woman,' for she was taken out of man."*
>
> *For this reason a man will leave his father and mother and be united to his wife, and they will become one flesh.*
>
> *The man and his wife were both naked, and they felt no shame.* Genesis 2:23-25

God thought up sex. He designed man and woman to be able to have sex. God gave us sex before sin entered the human equation. Sex is not dirty. It's not bad. But, it must be used in a God-given way—in a God-ordained context.

5. Why do you think it is so hard for our society to trust God's plan for sex? ⓨ-f

_____

_____

_____

_____

HUMANS, NOT HOUNDS

My wife and I have a Doberman Pinscher named Dolcé. One weekend I brought him to church, thinking he would be fine in my office during the worship services. Big mistake! The music started…Dolcé was fine. He was just hanging out in my office. Everything was great—until I began to preach. The walls between the auditorium and my office are thin, and in the middle of my message I began to hear Dolcé's distinctive, "Arf, arf!" But I wasn't the only one who heard it. The barks echoed across the entire auditorium.

I looked at my wife Lisa with that, "You need to get up there right now" look, and she made a beeline for my office, hoping to calm Dolcé down. But there was no calming him down. Dolcé wasn't thinking rationally. He didn't care that church was going on. He was simply responding to his animal instincts.

C. S. Lewis once said that when you remove morals from the human equation, you remove humanity from the human equation.

I'll say it again—we are not animals. Yet, so often people walk around like animals, enslaved to their sexual instincts to have sex anywhere and with anyone. This is most obvious with the men (sorry, guys, but it's true).

Have you seen these gentlemen's clubs? They call them gentlemen's clubs, but during this sexual revolution I want to change the name to kennel clubs. Places like that do nothing more than treat men like dogs, appealing to an animal-like sexual appetite.

When we take sex out of context; when we take this God-given gift and use it in a God-forbidden way; when we have little sex, what are we doing? We're going against the grain of God's creation. We're moving backwards from Genesis 1:26 to verses 24 and 25. We're essentially saying, "I'm not human. I'm an animal."

Do you know where the f-word comes from? The origin of the f-word is a farming term. It has to do with the mating of animals. We have taken that term and we have placed it on human beings. Here our great God wants us to be fully human. He wants us to have big sex and enjoy this phenomenal gift. Yet, we act like a bunch of animals.

Are you telling me you're a dog? You're not a dog. You are uniquely made in the image of God. You are fully physical and fully spiritual. We each have a specially created human soul given to us by God himself. That makes us much more than animals. ⓨ-g

6. Why don't you think more people recognize how little sex makes us more like a dog than human?

_____

_____

_____

_____

Not only does having little sex take us in reverse of God's creative plan, it causes us to strip others (no pun intended) of their humanity. Every day, in high school locker rooms, health clubs, coffee shops, and bars across the country people say things like, "I got a piece this weekend." "I'd like to get some of that." "Girl, look at that!"

What are they saying? "People are merely products for our consumption." It's a pervasive message in popular culture that bombards us everywhere we go. People are just objects to be used for our pleasure.

We lust and look at people as objects. We surf the internet and television channels for skin. We see an image or read about someone. And though we don't know the person, we strip them of their humanity and use them for our sexual fantasies. While we're doing it, we don't realize that we're stripping ourselves of our humanity. We're failing to recognize God in the whole picture. And because of that, we fail to see his image in either ourselves or the other person.

7. Why do you think sex is one area of our society where it is accepted to treat a person like a product? Ⓨ-h

_____

_____

_____

_____

Well, it's time that we turned the tide and started a sudden change—a change for the best. Our sexuality is something we are before it is something we do. It's not that we don't think about sex. It's that we need to think about it in a deeper way. God is the God of sex. He thought it up. It was given to us before sin ever entered the human equation.

In John 10:10, Jesus said, "I came that they may have life, and have it abundantly."

The word "life" in the original language means physical and spiritual life. It means full integration. It means hitting on all cylinders. And for us to do this, we've got to get the proper read on the gift of sex.

Sex is all about connection. It's about reflecting the nature and the character of God. So, whether you are single or married, it is my prayer that this study will help you realize your role in God's plan for sex. I pray that you begin to look at it through God's eyes and that some things will change in your life. It is my prayer that the sexual revolution begins with you.

8. Based on what you studied today, how would you explain God's stance on sex to someone who has never heard it?

_____

_____

_____

_____

SEXUAL REVOLUTION

WRAP IT UP

How does the sexual revolution begin today? It begins with you and your view of sex. You must first turn your heart over to God and say, "God, help me discover how big, how broad, how awesome sex is. Help me understand what you have planned for me when it comes to this great gift called 'sex.'"

Sex, it's a God-given gift that should be used in a God-given capacity. Let the sexual revolution begin today!

Prayer Requests:

SEXUAL REVOLUTION STRIPPED

Notes:

STRIPPED SEXUAL REVOLUTION

STEP IT UP

Take a step further over the next few days and spend some time reflecting on the following devotional thoughts that reinforce the previous session. Use these as reminders to take what you've learned and apply it to your everyday life.

DAY 1

Genesis 1:24

The Bible says that the earth was formless and void. It was chaotic. That was life before God spoke:

> *And God said, "Let the land produce living creatures according to their kinds: livestock, creatures that move along the ground, and wild animals, each according to its kind." And it was so.*
> Genesis 1:24

All through chapter one, there is a rhythm in the description of God's creative process. There is order, consistence, cadence. There is a purpose and goal. God's goal for us is to be fully alive. God provides boundaries for our lives to define purpose, provide clarity. Otherwise, without his guidance and provision, we would continue in confusion.

How can you see God's order in your life?

Ask God to help you listen as he communicates his order and purpose for your life.

SEXUAL REVOLUTION STRIPPED

Notes:

Prayer Requests:

DAY 2

Genesis 1:26-27

In our age of technology and commerce, if you want a painting by Picasso, Monet, Van Gogh, all you have to do is buy a print, an inexpensive imitation. If you want a Rolex, why spend the money for the real thing when you can easily by a cheap knock off that remarkably resembles the real thing. Reprints and remakes are available throughout our culture at discounted rates. It is easy to find a less valuable version of something made "in the image of" the original.

What our culture has done to sex is a cheap imitation of what God designed it to be.

Only humanity has the distinct characteristic of being made in the image of God. It is one of the things that separate us from the animals that God designed us to rule over. When we ignore our spiritual nature, we lower ourselves to the level of animals.

Don't trade your spiritual nature for the false promises of fulfillment living like an animal. Hold on to the value that God has given you by making you in his image. Recognize the spiritual side of your life that can easily be ignored. Live as the image of the glorious God that you were created to be.

Ask God to help you understand what it means to be made in his image.

SEXUAL REVOLUTION STRIPPED

Notes:

Prayer Requests:

DAY 3

Genesis 2:21-24

Adam had been surrounded by other living animals, but none of them were able to provide the connection and companionship Adam needed. God stepped in and created Eve. The result was something spectacular!

The Bible describes that man and woman become one flesh. That is a remarkable phrase. As a man and woman unite in marriage, they share something that connects them in a way unique to that marriage relationship. There is no doubt that intercourse provides a significant component to their unity. Their physical connection is combined with a spiritual connection that unites in a way God designed to enable two individuals to become one.

Sex outside of marriage is not an issue of the absence of connection as it is the absence of the value God created sex to have. When sex is experienced outside of marriage, the two compromise their humanity by becoming like animals. The act loses its value, becoming a scratch to an itch instead of an act of worship.

Ask God to give you an appreciation for the remarkable gift of sex and to show you how to protect your sexuality.

SEXUAL REVOLUTION STRIPPED

Notes:

Prayer Requests:

DAY 4

1 Corinthians 3:16-17

Have you ever turned on the news to see a story of about vandalism or arson at a church? It is amazing that even those who do not follow Christ recognize the significance of defiling a church. The reporters stand in front of the devastated sanctuaries or other structures and somberly report the damage with an air of indignation.

If those who do not follow Christ can recognize the sanctity of the sanctuary, why can't those who follow Christ recognize it? When we accept Christ, God places his Spirit in us. We become a sacred dwelling for the Spirit of God. Our bodies become a sanctuary. The biblical evidence is indisputable, yet many Christ-followers choose to ignore it.

Some Christ-followers think destroying their temple has something to do with piercings and tattoos. There is a physical aspect to us being the temple because God has given us physical bodies, but the spiritual significance cannot be ignored. We are not only physical beings, but also spiritual beings housing God's Spirit. Protecting the temple must have a more holistic view than just protecting our flesh. It means recognizing the physical and spiritual nature of sex.

Are there any decisions you are making that show a lack of respect for the temple of the Holy Spirit?

SEXUAL REVOLUTION STRIPPED

Notes:

Prayer Requests:

DAY 5

1 Corinthians 6:15-20

Corinth was a wealthy city with international influences. It was established in a strategic location for commerce so merchants, along with their goods, brought many religious philosophies. The result was a melting pot of ideas about philosophy and religion.

One of the famous religious influences in Corinth was the temple of Aphrodite. Part of the worship for this goddess included temple prostitutes. It is believed that there might have been as many as 1,000 temple prostitutes that descended on Corinth each night to practice their trade.

Paul knew Corinth was an area inundated with sexual temptation. Our culture shares that characteristic with Corinth. In the midst of those massive temptations, Paul warned the Corinthians about the significance of sexual immorality. There is something unique about sexual sin. Paul tries to explain it by pointing out that their bodies are temples of God as well as reminding them about the unifying nature of sex.

Have you ever played one of those arcade games where you try to direct a crane to pick up a toy from the pile of prizes? You waste your time and money trying to snag that one object of your desire only to discover the game is set up to take from you, not to give. Occasionally you can get a prize out of the machine, but the prize will never be worth what you wasted to get it.

That is sexual immorality. It takes and takes and takes with the promise of giving you the object of your desire only to eventually disappoint you. That is why God tells us to flee sexual immorality. Only God's plan can deliver sex in a way that fulfills not only your physical desire, but also your spiritual desire.

Where are you getting too close to sexual immorality and need to turn and run?

SEXUAL REVOLUTION STRIPPED

Notes:

Prayer Requests:

WEEK TWO

HEAVEN ON EARTH

START IT UP

Our culture continually ambushes us with sexual ideas and innuendos. Think about it. We drive down the freeway and see a billboard; we channel-surf and see a commercial; we flip through a magazine and see page after page of seductive ads. It's on the Internet and on the radio. Even our clothing can be designed to advertise sex. Sex is everywhere we turn. The world is saying, "Do it with whomever, whenever and however you want to."

1. What parts of our culture communicate the most about sex and what are they saying? Ⓨ-a

_____

_____

_____

_____

Our culture is screaming loudly about its idea of sex. It is not shy about the message. We are being blasted by images and ideas of sex all day long. But what about the church? Is the church communicating as loudly about God's plan for sex? For the most part, the message we hear from the church about sex is, "Don't do it. Don't even think about it."

Talk about some confusing messages! The contradictions create some serious tension. Do we deny the fact that we're created with a sex drive? Or, do we just surrender ourselves fully to our sexual desires? Or is there a balance in between those two extremes?

HEAVEN ON EARTH — SEXUAL REVOLUTION

TALK IT UP

There are so many messages about sex that it can be difficult to know what we should think. But that's the problem. When it comes to sex, many people aren't thinking right. And because they aren't thinking right about sex, they're having little sex. For these people, God has nothing to do with sex. After all, they will argue, it's just sex. **Ⓨ-b**

But God has so much more in store for our sexuality than "just sex." So when we think about sex, we need to think about God at the same time. One of the goals in this Sexual Revolution is for us to connect God and sex in the same thought process. Start with this thought: sex is between the ears before it's between the legs.

> Then God said, "Let us make man in our image, in our likeness, and let them rule over the fish of the sea and the birds of the air, over the livestock, over all the earth, and over all the creatures that move along the ground."
>
> So God created man in his own image, in the image of God he created him; male and female he created them.
> Genesis 1:26-27

We have to download this passage, because the way we think determines the way we feel, and the way we feel determines the way we act. God's goal for us is to be fully alive, to hit on all cylinders, to experience an abundant life. That includes experiencing sex his way. **Ⓨ-c**

2. How has following God's plan for your life allowed you to experience abundance in life?

_____

_____

_____

_____

SEXUAL REVOLUTION — HEAVEN ON EARTH

God created sex. Adam and Eve did not run behind some bushes, make love for the first time and emerge to say, "Hey God! Guess what we discovered?"

It didn't happen that way. God is the creator of sex. He thought it up. And he is pro-sex because sex is part of God's plan for our lives. So if you have a problem with talking about sex in the context of church, you have a problem with God.

3. Why do you think so many people struggle to connect God with sex? (Y)-d

_____

_____

_____

_____

THE CHURCH AND THE BED

For too long we've disconnected God and sex. In effect, we have taken the bed out of the church and kicked the church out of bed. It's time to get the bed back in church and the church back in the bed.

Why do we get nervous when we talk about sex, especially in church? Our problem goes back to not thinking right. Every time we think about sex, we should think about God. If the thought of that is a major mood killer, then you're definitely thinking about and most likely having little sex

God wants us to have big sex. Big sex comes from following the plan God designed when he invented sex. We can have sex in the marriage bed—one man, one woman—and reflect the nature and character of God. That type of sexual intercourse is worship. When we involve our mind, body and spirit, we mirror the Trinity.

However, we can choose to have little sex in the wrong bed. We can choose to jump from bed to bed and treat other people as products for our sexual consumption. But when we do that, as we saw in the last session, we are denying the fact that God created us as fully human. And we can sign ourselves up for some serious heartache and misery. The choice is up to you.

HEAVEN ON EARTH — SEXUAL REVOLUTION

In Proverbs, God warns us about jumping in the wrong bed.

> *Drink water from your own cistern, running water from your own well. Should your springs overflow in the streets, your streams of water in the public squares? Let them be yours alone, never to be shared with strangers. May your fountain be blessed, and may you rejoice in the wife of your youth. A loving doe, a graceful deer — may her breasts satisfy you always, may you ever be captivated by her love. Why be captivated, my son, by an adulteress? Why embrace the bosom of another man's wife? For a man's ways are in full view of the Lord, and he examines all his paths. The evil deeds of a wicked man ensnare him; the cords of his sin hold him fast. He will die for lack of discipline, led astray by his own great folly.* Proverbs 5:15-23

4. How could having the world's view of sex lead to extra-marital affairs? ⓨ-e

_____

_____

_____

_____

Marriage is a life-uniting act and a life-uniting covenant. That's where we can really be free and discover the depth and the mystery of sex. That's where we can discover God's ultimate plan for sex. And that's where we can fully enjoy this God-given gift.

GET RID OF THE PLATO

> *Awake, north wind, and come, south wind! Blow on my garden, that its fragrance may spread abroad. Let my lover come into his garden and taste its choice fruits.* Song of Solomon 4:16

> *...Eat, O friends, and drink; drink your fill, O lovers.*
> Song of Solomon 5:1

> *Do not deprive each other except by mutual consent and for a time, so that you may devote yourselves to prayer. Then come together again so that Satan will not tempt you because of your lack of self-control.* 1 Corinthians 7:5

When you read these verses, it is easy to see that God is clearly pro sex. He talks about it in ways that make a lot of people uncomfortable. Yet, if God is comfortable talking about sex, why are we so often uncomfortable about it? To get a deeper understanding, let's look at some church history.

The philosopher Plato, a man whose ideas and philosophies are evidenced throughout society today, basically said, in the area of sex, "The soul is good; the body is bad."

Enter the 4th century theologian Augustine. Augustine had some sexual problems and issues prior to becoming a Christian. Then, he took some Platonic thought into his theological writings—something that affected many people down the road.

Later on, enter the great reformer Martin Luther. Martin Luther also brought the anti-sex sentiment from Augustine and Plato into his thinking. And as he gained momentum, the church began perpetuating the wrong thinking and whispering, "Sex is bad."

And when you add it all up, you can see how over centuries the church has drifted away from God's original plan and ended up proclaiming (and believing), "Sex is a result of the fall of man. There's nothing beautiful or holy about it. Sex has nothing to do with God."

Here's the problem with that line of thinking. It's wrong! Yet, a lot of us have a layer of Plato on us that we need to remove because it's simply not biblical. God gave us sex prior to the fall, prior to sin. Sex is a good thing when it's done God's way because it's a God thing.

We don't think about Adam and Eve having a healthy sex life before the apple appetizer was served. For most people who were raised in church, our first introduction to sex was the story of Sodom and Gomorrah (and that didn't turn out too well).

5. Have you noticed the influence of Plato, Augustine and Martin Luther in your thoughts about sex? If so, how?

_____

_____

_____

_____

DON'T GET BURNED

There's something special about a nice, cozy fire in the fireplace, isn't there? You can curl up with that special someone, roast some marshmallows or warm yourself in the cold of winter. Sometimes in Texas, if it's even borderline cold, we'll crank down the AC just to have a fire in our fireplace at home.

Fires, when safely done, can be great. But what can happen if you don't manage the fire? If the fire gets out of the fireplace, even one errant spark can cause your entire house to burn down.

This marital bed is a fireplace. And sex inside that fireplace is special—it's romantic, intimate and hot! That's what God wants it to be. One errant spark, though; one errant flame; one move from the big bed to the little bed, and you'll get burned.

A lot of people could litter a room with little beds from their past. They've bought the world's lies about sex and slept with whoever, whenever and however. But all those sparks, all those errant flames have caused them to get burned time after time. And the biggest question when it gets to that point is, "Is God big enough to forgive me?"

The answer is yes. If you've found your life burned from letting those sparks fly, God can forgive you. But it takes a willingness on your part to think about sex and do sex God's way.

God wants us to experience the amazing gift of big sex. He wants us to see our sexuality against the matrix of his overall plan for our lives. He wants us to see it as more than "just sex." God wants to show us what it means to be fully masculine or

SEXUAL REVOLUTION HEAVEN ON EARTH

fully feminine. Whether we get married one day or remain single for the rest of our lives, God wants us to see our sexuality as something that impacts eternity.

Matter matters. Remember, we're fully physical and also fully spiritual. As a believer, everything we do, say, touch, and feel should be an act of worship. That includes sex. And when we choose to follow God's plan, sex becomes an amazing act of worship.

LIVING SACRIFICES

The way I think determines the way I feel; the way I feel determines the way I act. If I think like a dog, I'm going to feel like a dog and I'm going to act like a dog. If I think like a child of God, I'm going to feel like a child of God, and I'm going to act like a child of God.

> *Therefore, I urge you, brothers, in view of God's mercy, to offer your bodies as living sacrifices, holy and pleasing to God—this is your spiritual act of worship. Do not conform any longer to the pattern of this world, but be transformed by the renewing of your mind. Then you will be able to test and approve what God's will is—his good, pleasing and perfect will.* Romans 12:1-2

In the Old Testament people sacrificed animals on altars. The writer here says, "God wants us to be a living sacrifice." We can crawl up on the altar of our lives and humbly say, "God, I yield everything to you, even my sexuality." Ⓨ-g

And when I offer myself as a living sacrifice, my life is holy and pleasing to God, including my sexuality. That is my spiritual act of worship. That's why sex within the context of marriage is an act of worship.

6. What are some specific decisions you could make throughout your day to offer your body as a living sacrifice?

_____

_____

_____

Those of you who are close to my age may remember those toys called Creepy Crawlers? Basically, they consisted of some goo, a lead mold, and a pot for boiling water. When you squeezed the goo into the mold and boiled it, you could create all different types of creepy crawlers—centipedes, crickets, and all kinds of insects.

The world wants to squeeze us all into its mold when it comes to our sexuality. It wants to squeeze you into a little bed—a bed you weren't designed for. The Bible tells us specifically not to let that happen.

7. How have you felt the world trying to squeeze your sexuality into its mold? Ⓨ-h

_____

_____

_____

_____

RENEW YOUR MIND

Talk to a professional diver or a gymnast and they'll tell you, "Where the head goes, the body will follow."

The same is true when it comes to sex. Where my head goes (remember sex is between the ears before it's between the legs), my body will follow.

Where's your head? What are you thinking about? Are you connecting sex and God? That's right thinking. God wants to renew our thoughts so we will have right thinking. What are some things I can involve myself in that will renew my mind?

For one, I need to be involved in church. I shouldn't just show up on the weekends. I need to get involved in volunteering and serving within the context of the one entity that Jesus endorsed—the local church. Because when we step outside of ourselves and begin serving others, we will come in tune with God's plan for the rest of our lives as well.

Along with serving in the church, we need to renew our mind by reading, and applying, the Bible. When I do that, I align myself with God's will. This study is a great start to get you in line with God's view of sex.

Along with the Bible, we must also talk to God on a daily basis. Prayer is our vital link with God. And during those times of talking with God, we will learn to see our lives through his perspective.

Another key aspect to renewing my mind is my relationships. I need to hang around people who will encourage and challenge me and who will hold me accountable. I need to surround myself with people who will pray for me, love me, and affirm me. Are the people you are running with renewing your mind or squeezing you into a mold? Are they Creepy Crawlers or Transformers? Are they big sex people, or are they little sex people? The people we spend our time with will either help renew our mind to think right thoughts or push us towards little thoughts and little sex. And for singles and students, that includes who you date.

8. Take a self-exam to see how involved you are in the things that can help transform your mind:

- *Are you involved in any church activity besides attending weekend worship services?*

- *How often do you read your Bible? And do you simply read the words or do you look for ways to apply what it teaches?*

- *How often do you ask God for direction in decisions of your life?*

- *Do your closest friends encourage your relationship with God or pull you away from him?*

WRAP IT UP

This, then, is how you should pray: "Our Father in heaven, hallowed be your name, your kingdom come, your will be done on earth as it is in heaven." Matthew 6:9-10

In Matthew 6, Jesus told his disciples the pattern of prayer. "On earth as it is in heaven."

Now, as believers, we can bring heaven to earth. We can bring there to here by thinking right, feeling right, and acting right. We can bring heaven to earth through our sexuality. It can be an act of worship. What an opportunity!

We have a choice. We can either think right or we can think wrong. Where's your head? Because remember, sex is between the ears before it's between the legs. That is where the sexual revolution begins.

God,
 Teach me to think like you think so that I may experience your good and pleasing and perfect will for my life and my sexuality. Allow me to involve myself in things that renew my mind.

Prayer Requests:

_____

_____

_____

_____

_____

_____

_____

_____

SEXUAL REVOLUTION — HEAVEN ON EARTH

Notes:

STEP IT UP

Take a step further over the next few days and spend some time reflecting on the following devotional thoughts that reinforce the previous session. Use these as reminders to take what you've learned and apply it to your everyday life.

DAY 1

Genesis 1:28

God wants you to have sex. Let that sink in for a minute. It might be hard for you to believe based on what you have heard growing up in church, but it is true. It might be difficult for you to accept because you have never heard that in church, but it is true. God wants you to have sex.

God made Adam and Eve and then told them to go for it. God designed them uniquely male and female so they could have sex and then he encouraged them to do it. God told them to "fill the earth" which considering they were the only humans on earth – that is a lot of sex! Also, keep in mind that God created sex so the reason it is enjoyable is because God made it that way. He could have made sex a mundane routine like clipping finger nails, but he didn't. God designed sex to be an incredible experience.

The National Football League sets up boundaries for every football game, but that is not because they are against football. They recognize boundaries enhance the game. If there were no boundaries, the magnificence of their game would deteriorate into mess of blood and mud.

Just because God set up boundaries for our sexuality does not mean he is against sex. God wants us to enjoy that great gift in the best way possible. God's boundaries keep sex from deteriorating into a mess. It is God's boundaries that enhance our sexual experiences. Instead of fighting God's boundaries for sex, we should thank him for protecting the great gift he has given us.

What is a God-given sexual boundary that you have questioned or been frustrated with?

Take time to thank God for the gift of boundaries with our sexuality.

SEXUAL REVOLUTION
HEAVEN ON EARTH

Notes:

_____
_____
_____
_____
_____
_____
_____
_____
_____

Prayer Requests:

_____
_____
_____
_____
_____
_____
_____
_____
_____
_____

DAY 2

1 Corinthians 7:3-5

Avoiding sex does not make you more spiritual. There has been a false ideology floating through churches that sex is dirty and should not be talked about. It has suggested that sex is just for procreation. There is this idea that our sexuality is a bad thing. That is unbiblical at its deepest roots.

Paul spent the section before today's verses telling the Corinthians to "flee from sexual immorality" because of the dangers. Their sexuality could cause a tremendous amount of problems if they crossed God's boundaries for sex. Although Paul was teaching against sexual immorality, he was not teaching against sex.

Paul told husbands and wives to fulfill their "marital duty" to each other. The husband has a responsibility to fulfill his wife's sexual needs and the wife has a responsibility to fulfill her husband's sexual needs. Not only is sex a privilege, but also it is a responsibility.

As to the idea of avoiding sex for spiritual reasons, Paul attacks it. He gives couples permission to mutually agree to abstain from sex for a limited time, but then encourages them to get back to having sex. Paul did not want them to give up sex in a quest to be spiritual. He knew abstinence in marriage could actually do the opposite of producing spiritual maturity. Paul encourages husbands and wives to have sex for their spiritual well-being.

Do you see your sexuality in marriage as something that helps you spiritually, hurts you spiritually or has no effect? Why?

God designed sex in the context of marriage as something to benefit your relationship with him. Ask God to align your perspective of sex with his.

SEXUAL REVOLUTION — HEAVEN ON EARTH

Notes:

Prayer Requests:

DAY 3

Romans 12:1-2

Sex can be worship. Our physical acts can reflect a spirit of worship when we break free from the manipulation of those who do not know God.

God desires the actions of our lives to be living sacrifices to him. When we follow God's plan for our lives, we are worshipping. When we read our Bible, pray, sing to God, serve those in need, tell someone about the love of God or have sex with our spouse – we are worshipping.

God desires us to recognize the spiritual worship of our physical actions. God wants us to see that following his plan for sex results in worship. But, we will miss that opportunity to worship when we buy into the lies those who do not know God try to teach us about sex. There are many who claim to be experts about sex, but their advice can will only create confusion.

God wants us to break free from the non-biblical influences we have on our perspective about sex. Once we allow God to transform our thoughts about sex into his thoughts, then we can be free to enjoy sex not only as an act of enjoyment, but also an act of worship.

Ask God to show you where your perspective on sex has been influenced by lies.

SEXUAL REVOLUTION
HEAVEN ON EARTH

Notes:

Prayer Requests:

DAY 4

Proverbs 5:1-9; 15-23

We protect the things we value. We have security systems on our homes and cars. We protect our personal information by shredding documents and installing firewalls on our computers. We lock our car, lock our office and lock our briefcase to protect those things we value. The verses we read today are all about protecting something you value.

If someone came to you asking for large amounts of money to invest so they could keep the interest and keep a portion of your money, you would be crazy to let them borrow the money. Why would you invest your resources somewhere you are going to lose money?

That is the picture of investing our time and affection in adulterous relationships (any sexual relationship apart from a husband and wife). It just does not make sense. We waste our resources and never get an adequate return. We always leave those ventures with less than what we started with.

If we want a good return for our investment, we should invest in our marriages. Instead of daydreaming about a relationship with the woman in the next cubicle or the hunk from the romance novel, we should dream about what we could do to improve our marriage. Instead of flirting with coworkers and neighbors, we should flirt with our spouse. The time and affection we invest in our marriage will pay dividends that an adulterous relationship could never pay.

What resources are you investing outside of your marriage that should be invested in your marriage?

SEXUAL REVOLUTION
HEAVEN ON EARTH

Notes:

Prayer Requests:

DAY 5

Song of Songs 1:2-4

This entire book of the Bible is devoted to a relationship that most churches would label as scandalously sex. There are explicit descriptions of sexual desire and delight. Yet, this book did not make it into the Bible by accident. God inspired the words of this book and ordained that it be a part of the Holy Scriptures.

God's inclusion of Song of Songs should tell us something about his view of sexuality. God is not embarrassed about sex. He is not embarrassed about discussing sexuality in the church. God knew the Scriptures would be discussed in the church and home. He knew this book would be a part of the conversation. God wanted his creation to know his stance on our sexuality.

Most of those who grew up in church have never heard a message from the Song of Songs. It sometimes gets treated as a second class Scripture, but there is no such thing. Our sexuality is not a second class part of our spirituality. Just like God ordained Song of Songs to be a part of the Bible, God ordained our sexuality to be a part of our spirituality. We must embrace God's design if we want to experience God's blessing.

Spend some time reading more in Song of Songs to discover God's view of our sexuality.

SEXUAL REVOLUTION
HEAVEN ON EARTH

Notes:

Prayer Requests:

WEEK THREE

LEASHED

SEXUAL REVOLUTION

START IT UP

Imaginations are great. In an instant, by using your imagination, you can move from one place to another with no effort at all. You can travel to an exotic island, become a top-secret spy, or find yourself nestled in that cozy spot at home—even if that's not where you are physically.

One of my favorite places in the world is the Florida Keys, mostly because the fishing is phenomenal. At any point during any day, I can go there in my mind. I can see myself on a boat with the crystal clear water all around, a cool breeze coming in from the ocean, and a fly rod in my hand. In the blink of an eye, no matter what I'm doing, I can find myself fly fishing for tarpon. Without paying any money to actually travel to the Florida Keys, I can go there in my mind.

1. Using your imagination, describe one of your favorite experiences. (Y)-a

_____

_____

_____

_____

LEASHED SEXUAL REVOLUTION

Imagination is a God-given gift. Have you ever thanked God for your imagination, for the ability to travel somewhere in the blink of an eye?

Not only is our imagination a gift, but it's also a powerful force in our lives. It can be used to think God-honoring thoughts, to imagine God-honoring things. Also, our imagination can be used to conjure up God-dishonoring things. I can imagine good stuff and bad stuff, heavenly stuff and evil stuff.

TALK IT UP

When our imagination is connected to our sexuality, something powerful takes place. Jesus talked about it in Matthew 5. He had an interesting audience. Some of the people who were listening to him thought they were the paragons of purity. They pretended to have the corner on the morality market. And they assumed Jesus would applaud their morality and herald them for being so pure. After all, they applauded themselves.

But in Matthew 5, Jesus confronts this mentality and tells them to hold off patting themselves on the back.

> *You have heard that it was said, 'Do not commit adultery.' But I tell you that anyone who looks at a woman lustfully has already committed adultery with her in his heart.* Matthew 5:27-28

Ouch! Christ is saying that we can go to bed mentally with someone and commit adultery. And what we do with our imagination can damage our relationship with God.

> *If your right eye causes you to sin, gouge it out and throw it away. It is better for you to lose one part of your body than for your whole body to be thrown into hell.* Matthew 5:29

Jesus was talking about the cosmic ramifications of treating a person as a product. He was talking about the cosmic ramifications of turning a human into a hound. He was talking about what happens when we take sex out of context and reduce it to little sex. He was raising the bar when it came to lust. He took the Old Testament law against adultery to the next level. ⓨ-b

SEXUAL REVOLUTION LEASHED

2. Why do you think Jesus took lust so seriously, yet our culture does not?

_____

_____

_____

_____

GETTING NAKED

> *The man and his wife were both naked, and they felt no shame.*
> Genesis 2:25

Nakedness is a gift from God. Have you ever thought about that? Animals can't get naked. My Doberman does not ask me to turn my head while he puts on some gym shorts.

Nakedness assumes intimacy and trust. When we get naked in the marriage bed, it's not just a physical thing. It's a spiritual, emotional, and psychological thing. When a husband and wife make love, they're reflecting the nature and the character of God.

Our culture, though, tries to convince us that we're just a bunch of animals, that we should have animalistic sex. Because, culture says, sex is just sex. But when we buy into that lie, we are reducing ourselves to just small sex.

God says sex should be reserved solely for the marriage bed. And he has put a fence around that bed. But that fence is not there to control us. It's there to protect us and to free us up to discover the mystery, beauty and depth of doing sex God's way. Ⓨ-c

3. How could doing things God's way give you a new perspective on other areas of your life?

_____

_____

_____

SEXUAL REVOLUTION

We have to understand that God saved us from sin. But it doesn't stop there. God saved us from sin and for pleasure. Part of this pleasure is unleashed when we understand that we are uniquely created in God's image—masculine or feminine—and that we are to use our sexuality the way God intended.

LEASHED TO LUST

But what happens when we marry our imagination with our sexuality outside of God's will, outside of the marriage bed? The answer is lust.

Lust is a God-given desire (for sex) that has gone haywire. Lust causes us to see people as objects. And it causes us to use them for our sexual gratification, sexual buzz or sexual high. After we've stripped them (literally and figuratively); after the sexual hit, they become just another body to be discarded. And the cycle continues every time we lust after another person. Ⓨ-d

When we lust, we are not really thinking about the other person as a holistic individual. We are robbing them and robbing ourselves. We are stripping them and stripping ourselves of our humanity. And it always leads to pain.

4. How could being caught in lust lead to lifelong pain?

_____

_____

_____

_____

When it comes to lust, not everyone is in the same camp. Some people are recreational lusters. Lust will hit them now and then, but it's not a major stumbling block in their day-to-day lives. A scene in a movie, an advertisement in a magazine, or a person walking by on the street may feed a little bit of lust. But for a recreational luster, there are bigger issues in life.

There are also occupational lusters. You've rented some movies that you would not want shown on the side screens of your life. You've gone places, had conversations, read novels, magazines, or whatever that you do not want people to know about. You have a secret lust life, a secret thought life. You dabble in

SEXUAL REVOLUTION LEASHED

porn now and then, dabble in immorality now and then, and you're on the edge and the ledge of falling into the little bed that culture has made.

Then, there's another group I would consider as obsessional lusters. There's an entirely secret side to these people that no one knows about. You're spending thousands of dollars on pornography and prostitutes. The list is limitless. The obsessional lusters find themselves orbiting their lives around the little bed. They've bought into the lie that we are just animals. At the first sign of a sexual urge, this person convinces themselves there is nothing they can do. Sex is the most important need in their lives. But after the sexual hit or sexual buzz, they feel guilt, shame and remorse. They're leashed to the little bed of lust and their just dragging it through life.

5. What are the dangers of becoming someone who lusts more and more? What can you do to stop those dangers from becoming realities in your life? Ⓨ-e

_____

_____

_____

_____

Steve Hirsch, CEO of Vivid Entertainment, probably produces more pornography than anybody in the world. He has been quoted as saying, "Not only does hard-core porn not shock people today, but I think they want more—harder and harder and harder and harder."

That's a chilling statement against the backdrop of Ephesians 4:19: *"Having lost all sensitivity, they have given themselves over to sensuality so as to indulge in every kind of impurity, with a continual lust for more."*

Pornography and lust are directly assaulting God's plan for us laid out in Genesis chapter 1. God wants us to be fully human, fully alive and hitting on all cylinders. He didn't just save us from sin. He saved us for pleasure, for a purpose, for greatness. If I think big sex, which is God's sex, I'm going to feel big sex. Then I'll act out big sex, which is God's idea of sex—one man, one woman having sexual intercourse within the marriage bed.

LEASHED SEXUAL REVOLUTION

On the other hand, if I think like an animal, a dog, then I'm going to feel like a dog and I'm going to act like a dog. A lot of people think little sex is the answer. They are fine with minimizing sex and turning people into products. They don't think about the person they're lusting after. That person is someone's daughter. That person is someone's son. That person is someone's friend. That person is someone that Jesus shed his blood for. Lust causes us to miss all of that.

Lust leads us to chow down on dog food because we begin to think like and act like dogs. At first we think everything is great. But before long, after feeding on dog food—physically, mentally and emotionally—lust loses its buzz and we start to feel sick. We feel like vomiting from the shame, guilt, remorse, emptiness and anger that are the results of lust.

> *As a dog returns to its vomit, so a fool repeats his folly.*
> Proverbs 26:11

Remember, the way we think determines the way we act. If I'm thinking right, I'm going to act right. If I'm thinking wrong, I'm going to act wrong. I'm going to miss the purpose of life, the purpose of my sexuality, the purpose of what it means to be fully human.

THE LIES OF BEING LEASHED

Over the years I've talked to many people who've been leashed to lust and they tell me several things. The first thing is they feel unworthy of God's forgiveness. They feel like a bad person. But that's a lie from the enemy, because here's what Scripture says about you:

> *For you know that it was not with perishable things such as silver or gold that you were redeemed from the empty way of life handed down to you from your forefathers, but with the precious blood of Christ, a lamb without blemish or defect.*
> 1 Peter 1:18-19

Ⓨ-f How much is an object worth? The answer is not complicated. An object is worth what someone is willing to pay for it. What are you worth? Based on God's actions, you are worth the precious blood of Jesus. He died

SEXUAL REVOLUTION LEASHED

on the cross to pay for your sins so you could live in a relationship with God. You are worth so much to God that he was willing for Christ to die to pay for you. Ⓨ-g

Others who are leashed to lust say they feel unlovable. They think, "If others knew what I'm involved in, they wouldn't love me." These people are afraid that if others knew about the websites they surf, the clubs they attend, the conversations they have or the beds they sleep in, no one would love them. But that's not true either.

> *God demonstrates his own love for us in this: While we were still sinners, Christ died for us.* Romans 5:8

Did you catch the key part in that verse? God did not demonstrate his love once we got rid of our sins. God took the initiative while we were still sinners. He bridged the cosmic chasm while we still had our backs turned to him. Even if you are leashed to the little bed of lust, God still loves you. He loves you enough to want the best for you, even in your sexuality.

6. Using 1 Peter 1:18-19 and Romans 5:8, what could you say to a friend who is struggling with being leashed to the little bed of lust?

_____

_____

_____

_____

Something else people have told me about being leashed to lust is that they're unfulfilled. They say sex is the biggest need in their life. For them, it's all about sex. When they hear that God has a different plan for their sexual desires, they bolt. They are afraid following God's plan will lead to a sexually unsatisfied life. Once again, that is a lie.

> *And my God will meet all your needs according to his glorious riches in Christ Jesus.* Philippians 4:19

SEXUAL REVOLUTION UNLEASHED

Exchange the lies of lust for the truths told by God. Just call the enemy what he is—a liar! Embrace the hope there is for every one of us. We can have victory over lust, but it is not going to happen if we try to win on our own. That's why we have the church. (Y)-h

We're only as sick as our secrets. Many people are afraid that if others knew their secrets, they would be rejected. It's time for some men and women to put the church back in the bed and let go of those secrets. Walk into a Christian counselor's office and say, "Here's the truth about my life." Talk to a trusted friend who is a mature believer and tell them the truth about your life. Find that community of people who can help you, support you, and pray for you as you unleash your life from lust.

7. How have you experienced freedom by sharing a secret with someone you trusted? (Y)-i

_____

_____

_____

_____

It's also time to stop eating dog food. We need to stop feeding on the lies of the enemy. Instead of feeding on dog food, feed on the Word of God. Learn from God's Word both privately and corporately with others.

> *For these commands are a lamp, this teaching is a light, and the corrections of discipline are the way to life, keeping you from the immoral woman, from the smooth tongue of the wayward wife. Do not lust in your heart after her beauty or let her captivate you with her eyes, for the prostitute reduces you to a loaf of bread, and the adulteress preys upon your very life.*
> Proverbs 6:23-26

8. How has applying God's principles in the past been a light to your life?

_____

_____

_____

_____

When we lust, we become less than what God designed us to be. We're a far cry from living a holistic life. But there is hope. That's why we have the church. The church is a place for accountability, responsibility and encouragement. That's why we have God's Word. That's why we have one another. Christianity is not a solo sport, but for the luster it is a secret-laden life. To unleash your life from lust, get help from others and from God.

WRAP IT UP

C. S. Lewis, in <u>The Great Divorce</u>, wrote about a ghostly figure that carried a red lizard on his shoulder. The lizard, which was with him all the time, represented lust. Constantly and incessantly, this lizard would whisper seductive and sensual thoughts into the figure's ear. No matter how much this figure wanted to, he could not get rid of the lizard. And every time he tried, the figure realized that he kind of liked the lizard. It was comfortable. It was his pet.

One day, the figure made up his mind once and for all to kill the lizard. He had had enough of the guilt and shame and remorse, so he turned to someone else for help. An angel appeared and took the lizard off his shoulder and broke its back, killing the lizard in an instant. Immediately, this ghostly figure transformed into a muscular, handsome, distinguished gentleman. And the red lizard that had been killed suddenly became a beautiful white stallion. The man, with tears of joy streaming down his face, jumped on the back of the stallion and rode off into the heavens.

What's the point? When we kill the lizard of lust, it's not the end of desire. It's the beginning of pure desire. God wants to kill the lizard of lust in all of our lives. He doesn't want us to be leashed to lust. He doesn't want us to live like animals, but wants us to be fully human. It's time that we allow him to free us up and to lead us to the big bed he has designed for our sexuality.

Prayer Requests:

_____

_____

_____

_____

_____

_____

_____

SEXUAL REVOLUTION LEASHED

Notes:

STEP IT UP

Take a step further over the next few days and spend some time reflecting on the following devotional thoughts that reinforce the previous session. Use these as reminders to take what you've learned and apply it to your everyday life.

DAY 1

Exodus 20:17

Just a few commandments before the one you read today, God warned the Israelites "You shall not commit adultery." That is an easier standard to live by than Exodus 20:17 if you think about it. Adultery could be interpreted to be the physical act. That leaves wiggle room to commit a host of things that are still damaging without actually committing the act.

God wants to take the wiggle room out by clarifying the adultery commandment with another commandment. The word "covet" has to do with desire. It is the internal motivation that produces the outward action of adultery. The word Jesus uses when explaining the commandment about adultery is "lust."

Avoiding the physical act of adultery is not enough. Affairs happen in the mind and heart as well. The visual imagery created in the secret regions of our minds can strip the other person of their value. The emotional attachment may not be evident in physical acts, but it is a way we give ourselves to someone else. The damage of adultery can happen without the physical act ever taking place.

God's purpose is not to install rules to be worshipped. God provided boundaries to protect our relationship with him, our relationship with others and our relationship with ourselves. We can find strength and health by following God's rules when we seek God's desire behind the boundaries.

Are you being faithful to your spouse (or future spouse) by not coveting other men and women?

SEXUAL REVOLUTION LEASHED

Notes:

_____
_____
_____
_____
_____
_____
_____
_____
_____

Prayer Requests:

_____
_____
_____
_____
_____
_____
_____
_____
_____
_____

SEXUAL REVOLUTION

DAY 2

Job 31:1-4

Do you know the story of Job? He was the "blameless and upright" man who got caught in a cosmic chess match where Satan was trying to outplay God. Satan attacked Job by taking his family, his possessions and his health. If that was not enough, Job's friends tried to convince him that his misery was his own fault.

Job defended his actions as a "blameless and upright" man who had followed God's plan. In the midst of one of Job's defenses, there is the interesting explanation of a covenant Job made. He made the decision to not look lustfully at women. He made this with the understanding that nothing was a secret from God. Job's secret thoughts were not secret to God.

It is easy to think lustful thoughts are a secret matter. We think we can hide those little thoughts and control them. The problem is they are not a secret. God knows our most intimate thoughts and he will hold us accountable for them. They also have a way of working their way out into the public by affecting our relationships, our words and more.

God wants to protect us from the lie that our lust is a safe little secret. God knows the consequences of a "little" lust and he wants us to avoid that damage. The idea of committing to avoiding lust can be overwhelming, but by God's strength we can live it out.

Make that commitment with your eyes in segments. Ask God for the strength to make it all morning without lusting. If you make it, celebrate. Then, try to make it from lunch to dinner. Keep on breaking your day into chunks until you are succeeding days at a time on God's strength.

SEXUAL REVOLUTION LEASHED

Notes:

Prayer Requests:

SEXUAL REVOLUTION

DAY 3

Proverbs 6:23-29

Isn't it amazing how the very thing that will become fire in our laps can start out as something so innocent? The woman is described as having a "smooth tongue" which was an expression meaning she was smooth with her words or seductive.

The word used to describe "smooth" is interesting because it is related to a famous story – David and Goliath. David was the small shepherd with the big heart. Goliath was the larger-than-life warrior who opposed the Israelites. Each day, Goliath would march out into the battle field with incredible amounts of armor and weaponry to taunt the Israelites. No Israelite was brave enough to fight him… until David.

The small shepherd accepted the challenge and prepared to fight the giant. David was not dressed in impenetrable armor or armed with high tech weaponry. The Bible says that David had a primitive slingshot. Before the battle, David went down to the stream and chose "five smooth stones" (1 Samuel 17:40).

When David walked on to the battlefield, Goliath thought he could easily dispose of David. But, before Goliath knew what hit him, he was laying dead on the battlefield because of a carefully placed "smooth" stone.

The "smooth" words of adultery may seem like no big deal. We may assume we can easily overcome them any time we are ready. But, the truth is that our fate might be more like Goliath's. Those seductive temptations may seem harmless, but entertaining them is like trying to hold on to fire without getting burned. We can't be arrogant when it comes to adultery. If we want to avoid a giant defeat, we have to stay clear of the "smooth" words that tempt us.

What is an area of temptation that you need to avoid?

SEXUAL REVOLUTION LEASHED

Notes:

Prayer Requests:

LEASHED SEXUAL REVOLUTION

DAY 4

Genesis 2:21-25

God brought Eve to Adam and he was overwhelmed. Adam had been surrounded by the animals and none of them could provide companionship for him. Adam watched the animals live in community with their own kind, recognizing that he was alone. God saw it and stepped in to create a companion for Adam.

God took a physical piece of Adam to create a companion that was intended to be much more than just a physical connection. God designed Adam and Eve to connect in much more than just the physical sense. He designed them to be able to interact on emotional, intellectual and spiritual levels as well as the physical level.

God designed Adam and Eve from one flesh with the intention that they would unite back as one flesh in the context of marriage. Sex is a significant part of that bonding. It creates connections that go beyond the physical and reaches into the emotional, intellectual and spiritual levels that God designed.

God designed us to be able to stand before our companion naked, with complete openness and honesty, and feel no shame. The only way we can experience that kind of unity is when we follow God's plan for our lives, including our sexuality.

Is there anything you are participating in that could keep you from standing "naked" before your spouse and feeling no shame?

SEXUAL REVOLUTION LEASHED

Notes:

Prayer Requests:

DAY 5

Philippians 4:19-20

Have you ever thought about how capable God is to meet your every need? There is no need you have that God cannot fulfill. No matter how desperate the situation is or how dire it looks, God can provide for your needs. He has an endless supply of resources available if you will look to him to meet your needs.

For some, the idea that God can meet all your needs is new and incredible. For others, you recognize that, but there is something keeping you from becoming overly excited. You realize your life is more than just your needs. There are also the things you want. You need food, so if God gave you bread to eat everyday, your needs would be supplied but your appetite would be left wanting. So, there may be the lingering question about how satisfied you could be following God if all he meets are your needs.

Read Psalm 37:4

When we look to God to meet our needs instead of trying to satisfy ourselves, something incredible happens. God has a way of going beyond meeting our needs to the deepest desires in our heart. God has a way of providing true satisfaction.

God's plan for sex seems outdated in our culture. One man and one woman in the context of marriage seems almost impossible. Yet, for those who choose to trust God and rely on his plan for their sexuality, God will meet their every need in a way that truly satisfies their deepest desires.

Is there any area of your sexuality where you are not trusting God's plan and trying to meet your own needs and desires?

SEXUAL REVOLUTION LEASHED

Notes:

Prayer Requests:

WEEK FOUR

DO YOUR THING

SEXUAL REVOLUTION

START IT UP

I grew up in a family that was not afraid to talk about sex. For some of you, that might seem strange, but my family did talk about it. I remember when Lisa and I first started dating. We were 15, so I couldn't drive. When we went out, my parents would drive. They'd either take me to Lisa's or we'd go pick her up.

One time my father picked me up from Lisa's, and when I got in the car he asked me point blank, "Ed, have you kissed Lisa yet?"

I said, "Dad, I'm not going to tell you that!"

Dad was relentless. He said, "Really, man-to-man, have you laid one on her yet?"

What happened next might sound made up, but it is true. He said, "Well son, I want to teach you how to kiss a girl. First, you take her head in your hands and you begin to slowly kiss around the forehead and around the eyes. Then, you work your way down to her lips. And make sure to relax your lips." You can imagine how I felt sitting there listening to my father explain the intricacies of kissing a girl!

DO YOUR THING | SEXUAL REVOLUTION

1. How old were you when your parents talked with you about sex? What do you remember from those conversations?

_____

_____

_____

_____

Talking about sex can cause a lot of different reactions in people. Some are very uncomfortable with the subject. Others don't care when, where or even how they talk about it.

TALK IT UP Ⓨ-a

One of the reasons behind the *Sexual Revolution* study is that I want everyone—single, married, students, families—to understand the depth, mystery and greatness of sex. Because when we download this information, we can then teach it to others.

Most people think teaching their children about sex is all about "The Talk." But talking about sex is not just an event; it's an event followed by a process. Once a child is born and the doctor says, "It's a boy" or "it's a girl," sex education for that child begins. And it continues throughout that child's life.

Parents, we have to be the first sexual experts, the first sexual resources for our children if we hope to teach them about God's intention for the great gift called sex.

FOLLOW THE LEADER

When a child is born, the doctor hands the baby to the parents and says, in essence, "You're responsible. You're the leader. You're the one that God has entrusted with this child."

SEXUAL REVOLUTION DO YOUR THING

From that point on, we communicate with our children and we establish an environment where our children can learn. ⓨ-b

> *These commandments that I give you today are to be upon your hearts. Impress them on your children. Talk about them when you sit at home and when you walk along the road, when you lie down and when you get up. Tie them as symbols on your hands and bind them on your foreheads. Write them on the doorframes of your houses and on your gates.*
> Deuteronomy 6:6-9 ⓨ-c

2. How could you apply Deuteronomy 6:6-9 to teaching your children about God's plan for sex?

_____

_____

_____

_____

Teaching our children about sex is not a one-time thing. The training takes place in many ways over many years. Remember, we are teaching and training our children to leave our home and start one of their own. But, during the time that we have them, we're setting the pace, setting the environment for imparting God's truth into their lives.

Someone is going to teach your children about sex. God's design is for parents to take that initiative. From the time our children are born until they leave, we should strategically teach and impart wisdom to them. We need to supply them with a great foundation of God's plan that they can stand on when culture tries to paint the picture of little sex. We need to give them something to compare little sex to, and that needs to be God's truth. By doing that, we can create the environment where our children can come to us with their questions rather than turning to the wrong sources and getting the wrong information.

3. Growing up, where did you get most of your information about sex and how accurate the information you got? (Y)-d

_____

_____

_____

_____

    A lot of parents delegate the responsibility of talking about sex with their children without realizing the damage it can cause. They expect their children to just figure it out on their own somehow. Other parents are in denial about their children's knowledge of sex. I heard about one gentleman who didn't want his 14-year old daughter to hear about sex in the church because he just wasn't ready to talk with her about it if she had questions. But if we aren't there, our children will turn somewhere else. And sadly, by 14, your children may not know about sex from you, but chances are good that they know about sex.

    Since our children are learning about sex from a very early age, we have to be intentional about teaching them God's plan. We have to decide to start the sexual revolution in our homes. And remember what Deuteronomy 6 said. "These commandments that I give you today are to be upon your heart." It starts with our own understanding of big sex. Because only from there can we share the knowledge with our children.

    Our children are like us; they think about sex. Do you remember how curious you were as a child, a "tween" and a teen? Like with us, the issue is not that our children aren't thinking about sex; it's how they think about it. And it comes down to how deeply, respectfully and biblically we think about it and talk about it with them.

    The best place for our children to learn about sex is in the home. The second best place is the church. So we should partner with the church to teach our children big sex principles so they can avoid the pain and pitfalls that comes with little sex. Partnering with the church means creating an environment in the home where we talk about sex. And it means being proactive and intentional about being involved in the local church.

4. What were positive things your parents did to teach you about sex? Or, what you have heard other parents doing to teach their children about sex? Ⓨ-e

_____

_____

_____

_____

SACRED SPACE

Start early. Beat the culture to the punch when it comes to talking about sex. We should begin to have those conversations as soon as we see things that promote little sex. When you see something on your television or read an article that promotes a small view of sex, talk with your children about it. Explain the difference between what they see and God's view of sex. Tell them how our God is big, and that he has something better in store for them than what culture is offering. God never says "no" to sex. He simply says, "Wait until you are married." God wants us to see that sex is so precious that it should only be practiced in marriage.

Lisa and I had serious talks about sex with our children when they were in the third grade, but that was not the first time we taught them about sex. From the time they were very young, we began teaching our children that they were born out of our emotional, spiritual and physical love.

We also taught our children that our bedroom was a sacred place. We do not allow our children to sleep in the bed with us. Now, any parent will tell you that there are going to be times where your child needs you in the middle of the night. Every child will have a bad dream now and then. There are times when your children may not be feeling well. Those are exceptions to the rule. In our household, for the most part, our children have not been allowed to sleep in our bed.

> *Marriage should be honored by all, and the marriage bed kept pure...* Hebrew 13:4

I know it can be tempting to let your children sleep in your room, especially when they are infants. If you continually give in, though, just remember that you're taking away the sacredness of your room. Your room is reserved for you and your spouse. It is a simple thing, but it is creating an environment and respect for the marriage bed. It is a small action that sets the stage and teaches your children the larger principles about sex in God's eyes.

One time, Lisa and I took a trip with our twins who had just turned twelve. We got two rooms at the hotel—one for them and one for us. At bedtime, we sent the kids to their room, and Landra, one of the twins, looked at us and said, "Hey, Mom and Dad, do you have your own room because you want to go *do your thing*?"

I thought it was a good thing for her to say that because it shows that we have created an environment where our children understand the importance of the marriage bed. And they feel comfortable enough to be open and honest about their questions. We have taught our children that our big God wants us to understand and experience his idea of sex. We have taught them that God has placed a fence around the marriage bed for our protection, pleasure and procreation.

Guarding your bedroom is not the only way to emphasize God's plan for big sex. Things like Date Night also reinforce this. When our children were young, they would complain when Lisa and I would leave them at home with a babysitter while we went out. Now, though, they applaud it. They understand the importance of our relationship. And that is because we have created the right environment at home.

Don't get me wrong. We have not created the perfect environment in our home—not by a long shot. Our children still have issues. And we struggle at times to keep them in line with God's plan for their sexuality. But the important steps are there for them to feel comfortable talking about the gift of sex with us. They know that there is a major difference between what the world says and what the Bible teaches.

5. What are things you think are important to creating an environment to teach children about sex?

_____

_____

_____

_____

SEXUAL REVOLUTION DO YOUR THING

CREATING A "NEW LIFE" ENVIRONMENT

Some people may be afraid they cannot create an environment to teach their children about sex because of the little sex decisions they have made in the past. What happens when your children ask you about your sexual decisions before you were married, if you made little sex decisions? ⓨ-f

The foundation of Christianity is God taking us in our fallen condition and giving us new life. No matter what you've been involved in; no matter what you've done, God can and will restore you. If you have made little sex decisions, that provides you with a great opportunity to share with your children how God has restored you.

Don't give specific details. Give them a basic explanation of how you have made mistakes before, but emphasize how God has forgiven and restored you. Show that the result is, as a family, you're living for God and putting his standard above all else. Those difficult questions can be great opportunities to teach your children about God's forgiveness.

If we confess our sins, he is faithful and just and will forgive us our sins and purify us from all unrighteousness. 1 John 1:9

You can teach about God's forgiveness once you turn from your sins. But, if you are sleeping in the little sex bed, you need to do some work on your own life before you can hope to teach your children about God's plan. If you are single or a student, the decisions you make now will follow you into your future marriage relationship. Remember, we set an example for our children and many of them will follow our example—good or bad. ⓨ-g

INSULATION, NOT ISOLATION

When it comes to teaching our kids about sex, we need to think about insulation, not isolation. Sometimes people hear a message about sex and think they should isolate their family. They wonder if they should move to the mountains or somewhere else where no one can have any kind of influence on their family. That's not what the Bible tells us to do.

DO YOUR THING   SEXUAL REVOLUTION

My prayer is not that you take them out of the world but that you protect them from the evil one. John 17:15

Jesus was not into isolation; he was into insulation. Insulation gives us protection from the environment. We want our house to be a place of protection, a place of insulation. We want our children to know that we take our cues from the Bible. We should show them that we trust in God's authority to protect us.

6. What are some practical ways you could insulate your children without isolating them? Ⓨ-h

_____

_____

_____

_____

Another huge aspect of insulation is monitoring. I want to know what our children see on the Internet, television, and what they hear on the radio. That is part of monitoring what is going on in their lives. We need to get involved and know who our children are rubbing shoulders with. We need to know who they are dating. We need to be aware of what is going on in their lives, especially when they are young. Because the relationship patterns they choose at an early age will carry them throughout their lives.

Lisa and I have always taught our children that we should associate with all kinds of people because God loves every single person on the face of the earth. However, we draw boundaries about who they align with, who they hang out with on a more intimate basis. We teach them to associate with everyone, but to be careful who they align with.

We are careful whose home we allow them to visit. We monitor their friendships because we want them to align with people who have the same moral compass that we have. Our children may ask to sleep over at a friend's house, but if their family doesn't display the same value system as ours, we say no. But we say "no," with an invitation. We tell our children that they are welcome to invite any of their friends to our house.

SEXUAL REVOLUTION — DO YOUR THING

7. How well did your parents monitor you growing up? What did they do that was good and what do you wish they would have done?

_____

_____

_____

_____

The word "monitor" sounds so negative, especially in a culture that teaches that parents need to be best friends with their children. But monitoring our children is a key aspect to leading them. And it is our responsibility as parents to lead our children. We only have a brief window of opportunity to do that, so we must take advantage of all the opportunities God gives us. And the local church is an enormous part of it. From the time my children were very young, they have always been at church for services and activities—and that's not just because I'm a pastor. Our children are fully involved in the youth programs. To train our children in the way they should go, Lisa and I make sure we partner with what our church offers.

One thing that has been offered is purity ring ceremonies where the value of God's plan for sex is discussed. Then, students have the opportunity to make a pledge for purity and receive a ring to wear symbolizing their commitment. Many times the rings are presented by the parents to their children as a great way to involve parents in partnering with the church to teach God's plan for our sexuality.

God has given all parents the enormous responsibility of training our children. It is something we should take very seriously because God takes it seriously. And Jesus had some very strong words about leading children.

> *But if anyone causes one of these little ones who believe in me to sin, it would be better for him to have a large millstone hung around his neck and to be drowned in the depths of the sea.*
> Matthew 18:6 (Y)-i

Those words underscore the responsibility that we, as parents, have to not remain silent. Too often, parents remain silent when they hear others slandering

God's design for sexuality. If we do not speak up and teach appropriate things to our children, we might as well be joining in the slandering of God's design for sex.

WRAP IT UP

There are a lot of gifts we can give our children. And one of the greatest gifts that we can give our children is an understanding of God's view of sex. Show them the difference between the little sex they will be exposed to by culture and the big sex that our big God created.

Parents, teach your children with your words. Teach them with your attitude. Teach them with your actions. Because the revolution for them starts when you begin to teach them.

Prayer Requests:

SEXUAL REVOLUTION DO YOUR THING

Notes:

STEP IT UP

Take a step further over the next few days and spend some time reflecting on the following devotional thoughts that reinforce the previous session. Use these as reminders to take what you've learned and apply it to your everyday life.

DAY 1

Deuteronomy 6:1-9

What is the legacy that you want to leave for your children? Is it enough to leave them a large inheritance, or in your final days will you wish you had left them more? Leaving them more begins today. It starts with the direction we aim our lives and the decisions we make on a daily basis.

Moses told the Israelites that observing the commands God gave them would leave a legacy that continued with their children and the children after them. Something that lasting and beneficial does not happen by chance. It is a choice that must be made.

Moses told the Israelites to immerse their lives in these commandments so there was no part of their day left untouched. It started with the commandments finding a home in their hearts. This demonstrates more than just an external going-through-the-motions. It demonstrates a passion and embracing of God's plan.

Then, the commandments were acted out in every aspect of life. They were taught and talked about. They were placed in prominent positions and remembered regularly. The emphasis of the commandments would instill the importance of the commandments to their children.

This principle is for parenting in general, but it applies to talking about God's plan for sexuality. It is something that needs to be embraced by the parents and taught to their children. It must start in the heart and manifest itself in daily decisions. The principles must be made public to the children so they can learn to value them. Only then, will the legacy God wants to happen, happen.

Are you making decisions that will leave a positive legacy with your children's sexuality?

SEXUAL REVOLUTION   DO YOUR THING

Notes:

Prayer Requests:

DAY 2

Deuteronomy 6:20-25

The question may never be asked exactly as verse 20 describes, but there will come a time when your children question why you do the things you do. They will want to know the reason behind the principles that guide your decisions because those principles will be influencing their decisions.

God wants you to be able to tell them how living in a relationship with him has influenced your life. If that is going to happen, you must have a relationship with God. Your children will never believe you value God if they do not see the decisions of your life pointing to the value of God. Show them what a life in love with God looks like.

For some of you, the thought of your children looking to your life and asking questions is scary. Your history is filled with bad decisions and misunderstandings of what God wanted. Does that mean you are exempt from explaining to your children about the goodness of God's principles?

Notice that Moses described how the Israelites had been enslaved before God set them free. That stage of their existence could be used to emphasize the life altering power of God. The stages of your life that seem to be filled with darkness can be used by God to demonstrate his life altering power. That requires letting him shine his light into those areas. That also included embracing his forgiveness for the decisions of your past. And setting a course for the future based on God's directions. If you do this, it can make your life an incredible testimony to God when your children ask about the principles that guide your life.

What is a part of your life that you would be ashamed to share with your children?

Ask God to let his light shine into that area of your life. Embrace his forgiveness and ask for his guidance to set a different course for your future.

SEXUAL REVOLUTION — DO YOUR THING

Notes:

Prayer Requests:

DAY 3

2 Peter 2:17-19

Who is influencing your children? That can be a scary thought when you consider all the messages they hear on a daily basis. The scariest messages are not the ones that overtly oppose God. Those are easier to identify and avoid. It's the subtle ones that permeate a television show, the lyrics of a song or the theme of a movie.

When it comes to sexuality, there are a lot of influential messages. Your children will hear the promises of freedom that accompany those who oppose God. They will talk about undiscovered treasures that God's plan forbids. They will try to seduce like the serpent in the Garden of Eden.

How will you handle it when those around your children try to sell them lies? If you never teach your children the truth about God's plan for sex, they will never recognize the lies. Their education does not need to be a mudslinging campaign against those who oppose God. You can point out their danger, but focus on the brilliance of God's plan. Help them so thoroughly know God's plan that they can spot the counterfeit a mile away.

What are you doing to prepare your children to recognize the truth in God's plan despite the lies they will be told?

SEXUAL REVOLUTION — DO YOUR THING

Notes:

_____
_____
_____
_____
_____
_____
_____
_____
_____

Prayer Requests:

_____
_____
_____
_____
_____
_____
_____
_____
_____
_____
_____

DAY 4

If you are serious about protecting your children from all the false messages about sex that are so readily available, you have two choices. The first is to isolate them from any type of message. You can try to build an impenetrable bubble for them to live in. You can constantly modify that bubble and try to update it to protect them from the growing influences around them. That option can be tempting, but it is unbiblical. Check out Jesus' prayer for his followers.

Read John 17:13-15.

Jesus recognized there were differences between his followers and those around them. He recognized they would live in a hostile environment that could present many dangers. Yet, in the midst of his understanding he does not pray for isolation. Jesus prays for the protection of his followers. It is the second option for protecting your children – insulation.

Paul understood that it was not Jesus' desire to create some separatist community, but some of his followers did not. That is probably why Paul took the time to explain what he meant in the following verses.

Read 1 Corinthians 5:9-11.

Paul recognized that isolation was not Jesus' desire, but neither was ignorance. Paul drew boundaries for the Corinthians to protect them. That is insulation. God wants us to draw boundaries for our children that insulate them without isolating them.

Is there any part of your parenting where you are isolating instead of insulating?

How could you replace the isolation with insulation?

SEXUAL REVOLUTION — DO YOUR THING

Notes:

_____
_____
_____
_____
_____
_____
_____
_____
_____

Prayer Requests:

_____
_____
_____
_____
_____
_____
_____
_____
_____
_____
_____

DAY 5

Colossians 4:5-6

One of the reasons we should insulate is because it can lead to conversations with those who are not Christ-followers. They may want to know why we set certain boundaries for our children. The conversation might begin because they are critical of the decisions we make. It could begin because they are curious in the decisions we make. Whatever the reason the conversation begins, our response should be the same.

"Let your conversation be always full of grace...." God gave us grace when he took on the punishment for our sins and offered us life instead of our deserved death. He offered us the opportunity to become his children instead of condemned sinners. It was not what we deserved. God offered us grace.

We should remember that God offered us something we did not deserve. We should seek to use gracious explanations, remembering that we are not perfect and neither are our parenting skills. We should strive to offer them the same life and hope that God offered us. That means being humble with our explanations and focusing on helping them draw close to God instead of pushing them away.

However, our conversations are not to be just happy words of encouragement. That is the idea behind "seasoned with salt." Our gracious words should be seasoned with the truth so they offer true life and hope that can only come from following Jesus Christ.

By following God's plan of insulation, we will have opportunities to share the wisdom of God's plan. When we have those opportunities, we need to speak the truth in love so others have the opportunity to embrace the grace we were offered by God.

Pray that God will use the way you parent your children to create opportunities to share your faith with others.

SEXUAL REVOLUTION DO YOUR THING

Notes:

Prayer Requests:

WEEK FIVE

MESSED UP

SEXUAL REVOLUTION

START IT UP

In 2006, Justin Timberlake used a hit song to announce that he was bringing sexy back. The goal of this series, Sexual Revolution, is to bring the sexy back, though not the same way Justin Timberlake tried. This study is bringing the sexy back (and sex) back to God's original design. We're putting the bed back in church and the church back in bed. We're starting a revolution that God wants to happen in all of our lives.

1. What have you learned from this study that has impacted you the most?

_____

_____

_____

_____

Throughout this study we've talked a lot about the book of Genesis—specifically Genesis chapter 1 and 2. In these two chapters, God gives us basically one goal. He wants us to hit on all cylinders, to be fully alive. We've learned that we're fully physical and also fully spiritual. Another way to put it is to say that we're made in the image of God.

MESSED UP SEXUAL REVOLUTION

> *Then God said, "Let us make man in our image, in our likeness, and let them rule over the fish of the sea and the birds of the air, over the livestock, over all the earth, and over all the creatures that move along the ground."* Genesis 1:26

We're made in the image of God. We're uniquely male or uniquely female. In the marriage bed we have the nature and character of God merging when a husband and wife make love. There is a oneness, a mystery, a depth, an energy that is reserved for the covenant of marriage. So, we have a God-given gift—sex—which was given to us before sin entered the human equation. And we're to use this God-given gift in a life-uniting covenant called marriage.

> *The man and his wife were both naked, and they felt no shame.* Genesis 2:25

That's interesting, because if you're naked in a merely physical sense, you're ashamed. We want to cover our nakedness. That's why we wear clothes. Yet, before the fall, Scripture tells us that Adam and Eve were naked and they felt no shame.

Nakedness assumes intimacy. Nakedness was designed for the intimate setting of marriage. We're to get naked physically, emotionally, spiritually and psychologically only in front of our spouse. The Bible says repeatedly that we're not to take sex out of context. We're not to minimize sex. We're not to reduce sex into just a physical act. We're to keep sex big by following God's plan.

How do we keep sex big? We do it God's way and trust him. Our sexuality is something we are before it's something we do. And when God talks about sex to the single or the student, he says save sex for later. Don't have sex before you are married. Don't have sex with your fiancé, with you girlfriend, with you boyfriend. Don't have sex on prom night or any other night before your wedding night. Wait until you have this life-uniting covenant of marriage.

TALK IT UP

All of us are setting a course for sexual intercourse. We're either doing it God's way or we're not.

SEXUAL REVOLUTION — MESSED UP

2. Spend a moment silently thinking about what influences your thoughts on sex. Consider the people you hang around and the relationships you are in. What course are you setting for sexual intercourse?

_____

_____

_____

_____

If we set the right course for intercourse, we'll discover the full magnitude and mystery that God's gift of sex has in store for us. However, if we set the wrong course for intercourse, we'll experience some major problems.

Sexual sin is like no other sin. I've talked to a lot of people about all kinds of sin. I've talked to people who are involved in drugs. I've talked to people who have killed someone. I've talked to people who have robbed others. But there is no sin like sexual sin. It affects every area of our lives because the sexual nerve is woven into the very depth of who we are.

Sex is not just sex. It's a part of our mind, a part of our body, and a part of our spirit. We can't seperate those parts. Yet, people say, "It's just sex." We think we can park our soul outside the bedroom and just have sex. But again, there's no such thing as just sex.

3. How would you explain to a friend who was thinking about jumping in the little bed for little sex that there is no such thing as "just sex"? Ⓨ-a

_____

_____

_____

_____

Sex is never just sex. And in marriage, great sex is based on nonsexual things—romance, intimacy, conversation, environment. If you're involved in premarital sex, you're more concerned with the physical aspect of sex and you miss the importance of working on those nonsexual things. Then, when you get married, you run into problems because all of a sudden, it's not just about physical contact. And because you failed to work on the non-physical things, you miss the greatness sex can be.

Many people who make the discovery that great sex in marriage involves nonsexual aspects don't want to do the work. So they turn to things like pornography and lust. A lot of people—especially the guys—don't want to make themselves vulnerable. They don't want to get intimate. They don't want to communicate. They want it to be just sex. So, they channel-surf for breasts and butts, they go to kennel clubs, they feed on the lies of lust and have extramarital relationships. After all, they think, it's easier.

But taking the easy way is unnatural. We can't park our soul outside while we drive our mind and body over to little sex. When we try, we're abusing the Holy Trinity—God the Father, God the Son and God the Holy Spirit. We are also abusing the trinity of our being—mind, body and soul.

4. What are some practical things you could do to develop the nonsexual elements of your relationship? (Y)-b

_____

_____

_____

_____

MINE AND YOURS

I Thessalonians 4 has a lot to say about sex. But some people think the Bible is too archaic to be relevant. They wonder what it could possibly offer about sexual purity that would connect with our culture. They think sexual purity in biblical times was not an issue. And they assume the temptations in our sexually liberated culture are too different to relate biblical principles in an effective way.

But when the Apostle Paul penned I Thessalonians 4, the culture was much more decadent than ours is today. It was much more wheels-off sexually than

SEXUAL REVOLUTION — MESSED UP

our culture is now. One group that Paul was writing to had the Plato hang up we covered in week two. They thought the physical realm was bad, so sex must be bad. The other group was the polar opposite side. Many of them went to temples that promoted sex with prostitutes in the temple as worship. Men of Paul's day were known for having multiple partners. Homosexuality was rampant and much more. All of this set the stage for Paul's letter to the church in Thessalonica. (Y)-c

> *It is God's will that you should be sanctified: that you should avoid sexual immorality.* 1 Thessalonians 4:3

The word "sanctified" means to be set apart. Once we receive Christ, the Holy Spirit comes into our lives and redecorates from the inside out in order to set us apart from the world.

The word "immorality" in the original Greek is pronounced pornea. We get our word "pornography" from it. Pornea means sexual sin—things like premarital sex, fornication, adultery, and homosexuality. So, the Bible is saying that we should avoid sexual immorality. We're to stay away from it, to distance ourselves from it.

5. How could you distance yourself from sexual immorality without alienating yourself from people who need to know God loves them?

_____

_____

_____

_____

In my book, Rating Your Dating While Waiting for Mating, I compare our sexuality to a Ferrari. A Ferrari is made for the freeway. It's not made to go off-roading. If you gave me a Ferrari and I took it off-road, you'd think I was nuts! Why? Because a Ferrari is designed for a certain place and time and kind of driving.

God has given us this awesome gift called sex. Yet, instead of caring for that gift and using it the way God intended, many people take it off-roading and trash it. The Bible says our body is the temple of the Holy Spirit of God. So don't use his gift of sex to trash the temple.

MESSED UP SEXUAL REVOLUTION

> *...that each of you should learn to control his own body in a way that is holy and honorable, not in passionate lust like the heathen, who do not know God; and that in this matter no one should wrong his brother or take advantage of him....*
> 1 Thessalonians 4:4-6

First, Paul says be sanctified, to be set apart, to remain holy. Then, in these verses, he talks about not wronging our brother. It means that we should not take advantage of others. We should not put other people in a position where they would be forced to compromise.

That means that I'm responsible for my sanctification and yours. As Christians, we are called to be examples for others of God's grace, mercy, love and holiness. We are also called to help others be an example. So what I put into my mind, what I think, what I do with my body, my soul can influence other people's sanctification.

For example, the way women dress can influence a man's sanctification. Do you realize, ladies, the way you dress can cause a man to stumble? You can mess up his sanctification.

I'm not saying we should wear burlap sacks. I'm all for fashion. But where do faith and fashion collide? What do you show? Because what you show directly relates to who you attract. If you show your breasts and butt, you are going to attract guys that are focused only on breasts and butts. That's not what you want.

What you reveal is what you give away. And you can strip your soul when you strip outside of God's design for sex. You're abusing yourself. When you get dressed, look at yourself in the mirror and ask yourself, "Does this outfit glorify God?" If you can't make that call yourself, ask a trusted friend.

6. What do you think are some good guidelines for what we should wear and not wear? ⓨ-d

_____

_____

_____

SEXUAL REVOLUTION — MESSED UP

The Lord will punish men for all such sins, as we have already told you and warned you. For God did not call us to be impure, but to live a holy life. Therefore, he who rejects this instruction does not reject man but God, who gives you his Holy Spirit.
1 Thessalonians 4:6-8

There it is again. When we jump into the little bed of little sex, we are doing more than just damaging ourselves. We are rejecting God's plan for big sex and consequently rejecting God. We need to realize the seriousness of that decision.

ABUSES AND CONFUSES

Think about this. Some of you are doing stuff right now that two years ago you said you'd never do. And you're desperately searching for beliefs that justify your behavior. But no matter how you justify your behavior, it is still sexual sin. And there are consequences for sexual sin. There are physical consequences, like diseases or unwanted pregnancies. There are also consequences like shame and guilt from abusing your mind, body and soul. The bottom line is little sex abuses. But that is not all it does.

I have a terrible sense of direction. I remember getting lost on the way to the airport one time. Normally, people wouldn't think that's a big deal. But the airport was only 5 miles from my house! While I was driving to the airport, I thought I was going the right way. But I was lost—until my wife called my cell phone. She wanted to know why I wasn't at the airport.

I told her where I was and she said, "Ed, you're lost! Honey, you're confused. You need to turn around." I was confused and didn't know it.

Many people, when it comes to sex, are like that. They're confused and they don't know it. That's why they're confused. Hopefully, I'm like the voice of Lisa. I want to let you know, "You're confused. You're a long way from the airport. You need to turn around."

If you want to confuse and abuse your life, just jump in the wrong bed. But if you follow God's plan for sex, he will help point you down the right path, in the right direction.

MESSED UP SEXUAL REVOLUTION

Blessed are the pure in heart, for they will see God. Matthew 5:8

7. How can obedience in the area of sex affect your relationship with God?

_____

_____

_____

_____

God wants us to have a good sense of direction. He wants us to treasure sex. He wants us to understand the purpose and the power behind it. That's why he said, "Flee sexual immorality." He wants us to live pure lives. And there's a correlation between purity and seeing God, purity and discernment, purity and great decision making, purity and knowing what to do.

WHAT NOW?

You might be thinking that no one understands how much you have messed up sexually. You might be able to litter an entire church with little beds. You might be consumed with the memories of your past decisions. There is help for you.

God has done the work for forgiveness. And all you have to do is come to him and say, "God, forgive me. Cleanse me. I, Lord, want to receive your gift of forgiveness and turn to you."

Forgiveness is available if you want it. Think about how Jesus dealt with people caught in sexual sin—even caught in the act. He didn't degrade them. He didn't shame them. He simply told them the truth in love, nurtured them and said, "Go and sin no more."

Make a commitment for sexual purity. Just say, "God, today I'm stepping up and stepping out. You re-order and redecorate my life from the inside out." Tell God you want to pursue sexual purity and have big sex God's way.

That commitment won't be easy. It might take significant changes in your life. But remember, this is a revolution. Sin dealt with effectively is sin dealt

SEXUAL REVOLUTION MESSED UP

with radically. Maybe you need to cancel your cable. Maybe you need to cut off relationships that are causing you to stumble. You might need to resign from your job. You might need to move out the neighborhood or apartment complex. Maybe you need to throw away your computer. It could mean a number of things. But again, if we want to walk in purity and in freedom, we have got to be willing to do whatever it takes.

8. What are some decisions you can make to help you stay committed to purity? Ⓨ-e

_____

_____

_____

_____

Every time God tells us to make a radical decision he will phenomenally and richly bless our lives. He's not telling us to make changes just to mess us up, to keep us limited and stifled. It's for our freedom. It's for true pleasure and liberation.

Sin will mess you up. So make that commitment for sexual purity. Don't put it off. Your mind might be flooded with excuses why you should hang on to the little sex in your life. Don't listen to those excuses. Make the commitment today.

And once you make the commitment, back it up with action. Don't feed on dog food. Feed on the Word of God. It will set you free. Also, involve yourself in the local church. Involve yourself in ministry. Involve yourself with people who keep you accountable. When you do those things, you will have substance to back your commitment to remain pure.

WRAP IT UP

God has a plan for big sex. It's up to us to follow that plan. No matter what you have done in the past, remember that forgiveness is available. God will give you the power to revolutionize your life and he will cleanse your past.

Sex is a precious gift from God. We can thank God for that gift and honor him with that gift when we choose to experience sex according to his plan. God wants a sexual revolution in your life and he wants to use you to create a sexual revolution in the lives of those around you. Let the revolution begin!

Prayer Requests:

SEXUAL REVOLUTION — MESSED UP

Notes:

SEXUAL REVOLUTION

STEP IT UP

Take a step further over the next few days and spend some time reflecting on the following devotional thoughts that reinforce the previous session. Use these as reminders to take what you've learned and apply it to your everyday life.

DAY 1

1 Thessalonians 4:3-5

Passion can be a powerful thing. It can bring out decisions and actions that you never thought would happen. Sometimes passion can be harmless like a Jr. High girl writing the name of her crush on her notebook over and over and over again. Other times, passion can lead to destruction like a fit of rage that turns violent. Either way, passion is a powerful thing.

Some people allow their passions to drive their lives. They follow those feelings that well up inside of them and reap the consequences for many of their passions. Paul describes the people who do this as people who do not know God. If they truly knew God, they would desire his loving plan for their lives. As it is, they make their passions their god and follow them.

Sexual immorality refers to any aspect of a sexual relationship that is outside of God's plan. God wants us to avoid it all and choose a way that respects our bodies and the bodies of others. By God's strength, our bodies can be holy and honorable. That is, set apart from sinful passions and worthy of respect.

The transformation is possible, but it requires deciding who will be our god. We can make our passions our god and reap the unstable consequences of following them. Or we can follow God, who has proven to be trustworthy.

Ask God to show you if there is an area of your life where your passion has become your god.

SEXUAL REVOLUTION — MESSED UP

Notes:

Prayer Requests:

MESSED UP SEXUAL REVOLUTION

DAY 2

1 Thessalonians 3:6-8

Why is God concerned with not letting our passions control our lives? God recognizes that when our passions rule our lives, the result is total chaos in the lives of others. If our focus is fulfilling our passions, we will take advantage of those around us. We will treat them as products to fulfill our passions and ignore their value.

King David lived parts of his life fulfilling his passions. Each time, it created consequences for him, but it also led to consequences in his family. David had multiple wives and children with the multiple wives as a result of David pursuing his own passions.

Read 2 Samuel 13:1-2

Amnon was being driven by his passions so much so that it made him ill. A friend told Amnon to follow his passions and devised a plan to help him. Amnon tricked his sister Tamar into his bedroom. When Tamar pleaded with him to let her go, Amnon listened to his passions instead of Tamar.

Read 2 Samuel 13:14-15

Amnon followed his passions. He deceived and wounded his sister. He brought shame to his family. He committed a horrible offense, and discovered that his passions made a poor god. In the end, Amnon found no satisfaction in following his passions. It actually led him to hate his sister even more than he loved her.

The damage did not end there. Tamar had a brother named Absalom. When Absalom found out what Amnon had done, he became furious. This lead to a plot devised by Absalom to murder Amnon, further damaging David's family.

Each person was led by his own passions instead of following God. The result was hurt and devastation beyond description.

How have you followed your passions and hurt someone else?

SEXUAL REVOLUTION MESSED UP

What passions are you following now that could hurt you and those around you?

Notes:

_____
_____
_____
_____
_____
_____
_____
_____
_____

Prayer Requests:

_____
_____
_____
_____
_____
_____
_____
_____
_____
_____

MESSED UP SEXUAL REVOLUTION

DAY 3

Proverbs 14:12

Have you ever been lost, but sure that you knew the right way to go? In confidence, you continue down a path leading you in the wrong direction. If you took the time to look around, you could notice indicators that you were off track.

Then comes the realization that you are lost. But you're still determined to find your way out. Just one more mile, or one more turn – both in hopes of something changing and a new direction appearing.

"There is a way that seems right..." in relationships, finances, even sexuality. But, as many have found out, that way leads to death. It has severed relationships, sunk finances and used our sexuality in ways God never intended. Despite all the damage we have seen it do, that way can still be tempting.

Read John 10:10

The way that seems right is built by the same one who came to steal, kill and destroy; but there is another option. There is a way provided by the one who said he is The Way (John 14:6). It is not too late to leave the way that seems right. Jesus opened the way to an abundant life and invites us to join him.

Why do you think the way that ends in death is still so appealing?

What is an area where you are following the way that seems right instead of following The Way?

SEXUAL REVOLUTION — MESSED UP

Notes:

Prayer Requests:

MESSED UP SEXUAL REVOLUTION

DAY 4

Hosea 1:2

How does it make you feel to read that God told one of his faithful prophets to take an adulterous wife? That is outrageous that God would expect someone who was faithful to him to live with a spouse who was unfaithful. Think about the hurt that would be experienced in that relationship. Think about the damage that would be done when the adultery took place. Hosea would know all of this going in to the relationship. How could Hosea stand there and make vows of love and commitment on his wedding day when he knew his bride would cheat on him?

God told Hosea to do this as a picture of what the Israelites were doing to God. They had cheated on God with other gods and given their love and affection away in an adulterous fashion. In God's wisdom, he knew what would happen when he rescued the Israelites from slavery hundreds of years before. God knew they would cheat on him. God knew they would be adulterous with their affection. Yet, God showed them faithful love.

Read Hosea 3:1-3

After the adultery, Hosea showed his wife love again. Hosea actually purchased his wife from her adulterous ways. The amount Hosea paid was around the price paid for a slave. Hosea rescued his adulterous wife from her enslavement. She did not deserve it, yet Hosea paid a great price so he could love his unfaithful wife.

This is a picture of what God has done for us. We have been unfaithful to him. We have been adulterous in the sense that we have followed our own plans. Yet, God paid an incredible price through Jesus Christ so that he could live in a love relationship with us. It does not matter how far we have become enslaved to sin, God desires to free us and love us.

If God was willing to take on that burden so that he could love us, what does that communicate about his desires/commands for our lives?

SEXUAL REVOLUTION — MESSED UP

Notes:

Prayer Requests:

DAY 5

Hebrews 13:4

The author of Hebrews is making some concluding remarks in the form of practical advice. He speaks about hospitality, sympathy, finances and leadership. In the middle of all these is a remark about marriage that could easily be overlooked. "Marriage should be honored by all…." It is not just the remark that commonly gets overlooked, it is the principle that also gets ignored. Very rarely is marriage honored.

In a society where people get married for whimsical reasons and half of all marriages do not last, it does not sound like marriage is being honored. The word "honored" carries the idea of something cherished and respected. We should see marriage as a cherished and valued commodity like a rare gem.

When marriage is seen with this proper value, the marriage bed – that most intimate of places – increases in value. This means more than protecting the actual bed. It is a call to protect the spiritual act of sex. As an intimate part of this honored institution, it deserves to be more than the punch line of a joke or a moment of lustful weakness.

What do you do that shows you honor marriage? This verse was not written just to married people so if you are single, it applies to you as well. What are you doing to show that marriage is a cherished and valuable institution? And in addition, are you protecting the intimate act of sex that is reserved for the sacred covenant of marriage?

What changes could you make this week to demonstrate you honor marriage and desire to keep the marriage bed protected?

SEXUAL REVOLUTION — MESSED UP

Notes:

_____
_____
_____
_____
_____
_____
_____
_____
_____
_____

Prayer Requests:

_____
_____
_____
_____
_____
_____
_____
_____
_____
_____
_____
_____

LEADER'S GUIDE
SESSION ONE

WHEN FAITH HAS LOST ITS FIZZ

LEADER'S NOTES

1. **Of all the changes in our world since the 1960's, which ones do you think have been the best and worst?**

    Ⓨ-a For many students, the bed is not the most common association with sex. It might be worth discussing what imagery brings immediate thoughts about sex. For example, the back seat of a car or a back room at a party. And, if those images are more associated with sex than a bed, what does that communicate about the way students see sex?

2. **Growing up, what did you learn about sex – either from your parent or your church?**

    Most people probably grew up in a home or church where sex wasn't talked about at all, or it was talked about in a negative way (i.e. don't do it). Encourage your group to share how those viewpoints on sex affected how they felt about it. Maybe they felt it was dirty and were scared of it, or maybe the felt like it was forbidden fruit and that made it more appealing.

    Ⓨ-b If your parents or your church did not talk much about sex, what did that communicate to you about sex and how has that affected your ability to talk with your parents or people at church about sex?

3. **Why do you think God designed sex for the context of marriage and not as a gift to be shared flippantly?**

    Tip: Encourage your group to think about the negative consequences of sex outside the marriage bed as well as the positive results of having a strong sexual relationship within the confines of marriage.

STRIPPED SEXUAL REVOLUTION

Ⓨ-c *One visual you could use is to bring several colors of Play-Dough and squish the different colors together, then try to separate them. Once the colors have been mixed, it is virtually impossible to separate them. Sex shares parts of us that are virtually impossible to separate after we break up. That is why sex was designed for one partner in the context of a committed marriage.*

Another illustration is to bring items like a used toothbrush, chewed gum, used deodorant, etc. Ask them how many of them would like to share these objects with someone else. We wouldn't share these things, but we will share something far more valuable like our sexuality. It shows how little value we place on our sexuality.

4. What do you think it means to be made in the image of God?
God made us in his image meaning that we are both physical and spiritual beings. There is something more to us than the flesh and bones we can touch. There is a part of us that is connected to our thoughts, feelings and identity. That part is the spiritual side and cannot be disconnected from the physical flesh we live in.

Ⓨ-d *As you discuss what it means to be made in the image of God, think about how valuable that makes us. We need to recognize our value as the image of God because that will impact our decisions about sexuality. If we do not value ourselves, we will be more likely to give ourselves away sexually.*

Ⓨ-e *God's plan for big sex involves one woman, one man, in the context of marriage. That is God's recipe for sex and when you remove one of those ingredients, the outcome is not the same. You could illustrate this by baking cookies without sugar or bread without yeast.*

5. Why do you think it's so hard for our society to trust God's plan for sex?
It's hard for our society to trust God's plan for sex because we are not exposed to it. The world's plan for sex is all around us in the media. We're bombarded with so many sexual images that little sex has become the norm and Godly sex is a mystery to most people. With so few examples of people living out God's plan for sex, it is hard to trust his plan.

Ⓨ-f *For many students, it is a curiosity issue. They are curious because of all the things they have heard about sex from popular culture. Also, when sex becomes a forbidden topic of discussion at home, that can create curiosity as well. When it comes to curiosity about sex, it is a trust issue. We have to learn to trust God so we do not let our curiosity control us.*

Ⓨ-g *Acting like hounds can be less of an issue of self-control and more of an issue of what we want. For example, some guys might say that cannot control their sexual*

SEXUAL REVOLUTION STRIPPED

desires, but that is not true. If they were about to have sex and their girlfriend's dad walked in, they could control their sexual urges.

6. Why don't you think more people recognize how little sex makes us more like a dog than human?

Dogs act on instinct and desire, while humans have the unique gifts of knowledge, understanding, and free will. Neglecting those gifts requires checking your brain at the door and acting on impulses alone. Taking your brain out of the equation is how you can act like a dog without realizing it.

Also, it could be that many people do not care that they are acting like a dog. They do not see the value in acting like a human instead of acting like a dog.

7. Why do you think sex is one area of our society where it is accepted to treat a person like a product?

Fantasizing about a person might seem like no harm is being done to them, especially when they actually want to be lusted over. People take compromising roles in movies, pose seductively in photo shoots, and dress in a way that is intended for sexual attention. It may seem like lust is acceptable in those situations because the person is soliciting it, but not everyone wants to be seen in that way. People make the assumption that because some men and women want to be seen in that way, all men and women want to be seen in that way.

(Y)-h It is not just an issue of treating the other person as a product. It can also be an issue of letting ourselves be treated like a product. For some reason, we are willing to become objects when it comes to sexuality when we would never let ourselves be treated like objects in other areas of life.

8. Based on what you studied today, how would you explain God's stance on sex to someone who has never heard it?

Tip: Help your group to think of ways to get their point across without seeming judgmental. Encourage them to not only talk about what they should say, but also why it's important to say it. They might be the one person who can get through to their friend and save them from a lot of pain and hardship. If anyone in your group has a friend they need to share God's stance on sex with, suggest that they pray for God to give them the right words at the right time.

STRIPPED SEXUAL REVOLUTION

CREATIVE NOTES

ICEBREAKERS

Under the Influence

Discuss the images you have seen on television, in movies, in magazines and other places that have been influenced by the sexual revolution that began in the 1960s.

BRIDGE – Over the past 40 years, the sexual revolution has been very influential. God desires to begin an equally influential sexual revolution that points people to his plan for sex.

Popular Culture Church

Brainstorm images from popular culture that portray the church's stance on sex. The images can include television and movie characters, songs, public figures, etc. Compare how many images communicate the church is against sex and how many images communicate the church is for sex.

BRIDGE – The church is known for being against sex, but God is not against sex. It is time we put the bed back in the church and the church back in the bed.

Revolution Defined

Take a minute and let each person write their own definition of "revolution" then compare the different definition.

BRIDGE – God wants to unite us under his design of sex to bring about a true revolution.

Buying a Bed

How old were you when you bought your first bed as an adult (or if you are married – as a couple)? What factors influenced your decision to purchase the bed you did?

BRIDGE – Choosing a bed can be a big decision. God wants us to choose the bed of big sex which follows his plan instead of the bed of little sex that follows society's plan.

HANDS-ON ACTIVITIES

Cheap Imitation

Pass out blank sheets of paper and crayons. Then, show a famous painting like the Mona Lisa. Tell the group they have two minutes to reproduce the famous painting.

SEXUAL REVOLUTION STRIPPED

Show the reproductions and compare them to the original.

BRIDGE – God designed sex. Anything outside of his plan is just a cheap imitation that cannot compare to the beauty and brilliance of the original design.

Pick Up Lines

Pass out slips of paper to everyone in the group and ask them to write down pick up lines they have heard. Put all the slips of paper in a hat and pass the hat around the group. Everyone has to choose one and read it to the group. Discuss the pick up lines and what they communicate about the people they are said to and the people who said them.

BRIDGE – God wants us to recognize that we are not animals. He wants us to see others as humans and appreciate the way he has designed them.

Hot Terms

On a piece of paper, write down as many terms as you can think of that describe someone who is attractive. Then, divide a piece of poster board into two columns. On top of one column write "Object" and on top of the other column write "Human." Transfer the terms for attractive into the two columns based on if they emphasize the person as an object or takes into account their humanity.

BRIDGE – God wants us to see each other as more than objects. His plan is for us to be fully human and recognize the humanity of others.

VISUAL REINFORCEMENTS

Bringing the Bed Back

If you have a bedroom large enough to accommodate your group, meet in the bedroom for this week to emphasize bringing the bed back.

Cover Shot

Bring three different magazines and discuss if the covers feed God's desire for us to be fully human or the mindset that we are animals (be selective in the magazines you choose to not show anything inappropriate).

Not an Animal

Put out animal masks as a reminder that when we give in to "animal instincts" we are being something we were not designed to be.

STRIPPED SEXUAL REVOLUTION

MEDIA REINFORCEMENTS

Revolution by the Beatles

The song is based on being cautious of the revolutions some people want to institute.

Who Let the Dogs Out by Baha Men

The song describes how some people can act like dogs.

TAKE HOME OBJECT

Animal Crackers

Pass out animal crackers as a reminder that God did not create us to be animals.

Sand Paper

In our culture, it is easy to have some rough edges in our view of sex. God wants to shape our view of sex and smooth out the rough edges.

LEADER'S GUIDE
SESSION TWO

HEAVEN ON EARTH

LEADER'S NOTES

1. **What parts of our culture communicate the most about sex and what are they saying?**

    Tip: Your group will probably have lots of answers to where sexual messages are coming from, but encourage them to dig deeper into the second part of the question. What is the theme of these sexual messages? What do they say to married people, singles, children or teenagers?

    (Y)-a *Brainstorm commercials that try to use sexuality to sell their product. Or, try to brainstorm female pop singers that do not use their sexuality to sell their music. What is the ratio of those who do not use their sexuality to those who do? What does that say about the influence of sexuality in our culture?*

    (Y)-b *God and sex do not seem to go together, but they are actually a great combination. What are other combinations that seem unusual at first, but actually go together well? For example: peanut butter and bananas, ranch dressing and pizza, fries and milkshakes (For a visual, make some of these snacks to let the students try).*

    (Y)-c *If you see people as products, you will not feel guilty for using them as products. You will use them sexually then discard them once you are fulfilled with little regard for their well-being.*

HEAVEN ON EARTH SEXUAL REVOLUTION

2. How has following God's plan for your life allowed you to experience abundance in life?

Encourage your group to think of several areas of abundance. Abundance can come in the form of finances, friendships, family, or even abundant peace during difficult times.

3. Why do you think so many people struggle to connect God with sex?

Many in your group have probably spent their lives viewing sex as bad or dirty, so learning to see it as Godly and beautiful is a major change. Others may not think of sex in a negative way, but they haven't learned about it in church. People struggle to connect God with sex because the two are not usually talked about in the same conversation, other than to say that God doesn't want you to have sex before marriage.

Ⓨ-d *What are images from our culture (ie: movies, television, music, etc.) that make it look like God is against sex?*

4. How could having the world's view of sex lead to extramarital affairs?

The world's view is that sex is "just sex" and that makes it easy to rationalize that it's not a big deal. People buy the lie that they can keep their family life separate from their sex life, but the truth is that sexual affairs don't stay hidden forever and they destroy marriages and families all the time.

Ⓨ-e *Many students are watching their parents go through this right now. Consider using an alternative question like, "How have you seen sex affect your friends' relationships?" or "How has someone's sexual sin affected you?" to keep from bringing up hurt that is unnecessary.*

Also explain that adultery, in a larger sense, is sex with someone that is not our spouse. So, when a single person has sex with someone that is not their spouse, they are breaking the principle behind God condemning adultery.

5. Have you noticed the influence of Plato, Augustine and Martin Luther in your thoughts about sex? If so, how?

Plato's views on sex were that it was dirty and bad, and many in your group probably grew up thinking that way. Challenge your group to consider some of the first words that come to mind when they hear the word "sex." Is God one of those words? If not, Plato's influence is probably there.

Ⓨ-f *Bring something that has been partially burned as a visual for the damage that can be caused when we let sexual sparks out of the marriage bed.*

Ⓨ-g *There is a saying that the problem with being a living sacrifice is that we can crawl off the alter. In other words, being a living sacrifice is a continual choice.*

SEXUAL REVOLUTION HEAVEN ON EARTH

6. What are some specific decisions you could make throughout your day to offer your body as a living sacrifice?

In a sexual sense, there are many ways to offer your body as a living sacrifice. Some examples are abstaining from sex outside the marriage bed, having sex often inside the marriage bed, abstaining from masturbation and lustful thoughts, and dressing in a way that does not attract sexual attention from others. Offering your body as a living sacrifice goes beyond sex, though. Other ways you could offer your body as a living sacrifice include: the words you use, the way you serve others, how you comfort those who are hurting, the foods and beverages you consume, etc.

7. How have you felt the world trying to squeeze your sexuality into its mold?

Our society and mass media can shape our sexuality if we're not careful. Casual sex on TV shows and movies can influence our thoughts about sex, and so can song lyrics, advertisements, books, and magazine articles. It's important for us to keep our minds on God and to arm ourselves with his word so that we can recognize and flee from the sexual messages that surround us every day.

Y-h *What can you do to stop the squeeze?*

8. Take a self-exam to see how involved you are in the things that can help transform your mind:

Tip: Instruct your group to spend time alone thinking about their answers to these questions. This will help them to see if they're doing all the right things for God to be able to renew their minds and transform their lives.

HEAVEN ON EARTH SEXUAL REVOLUTION

CREATIVE NOTES

ICEBREAKERS

Speak No Evil

Sex is a prevalent part of our society. It seems like many times, everyone but the church is talking about sex. Why do you think so many Christ-followers struggle with talking about sex?

BRIDGE – God invented sex so it is not something to be ashamed of. The church and Christ-followers should talk about sex so others can learn about God's plan.

Mixed Messages

We live in a society that sends lots of mixed messages. Beer companies show advertisements with wild parties then follow it by saying "please drink responsibly." Bosses demand things of their employees that they do not demand of themselves. What are other examples of mixed messages you have noticed?

BRIDGE – For a long time, the church has sent mixed messages about sex. They have said, "Sex is bad" yet sex is a gift from God. We need to understand God is for sex. He wants us to experience it in its fullest sense, which comes from following his plan.

HANDS-ON ACTIVITY

Jenga

Play the game Jenga where you remove pieces until the tower falls.

BRIDGE – Little sex gives away pieces of who we are and leads to a personal fall.

Wrong Way

Have contests with your group to use utensils and tools in ways they were not designed for. For example: peel potatoes with a spoon, use a fork to scoop water from one bowl to another, use a screwdriver to hammer a nail, etc.

BRIDGE – God designed sex with specific purposes in mind. When we use sex apart from God's design, it will leave us disappointed.

Pass the Plastic Cup

Serve drinks in plastic cups and write the name of each person on their cup. During

SEXUAL REVOLUTION — HEAVEN ON EARTH

the lesson, discuss how many people would be comfortable if everyone traded cups and drank after someone else.

BRIDGE – Most of us would have a problem sharing a plastic cup with someone else, even if we know them well. Yet, many people will share something much more personal in sex, and not think twice about it.

VISUAL REINFORCEMENTS

One Knife, Three Sandwiches

Tell your group you are going to make three different sandwiches. One will have peanut butter and jelly, one will have a meat and mayo and one will have a meat and mustard. As you make the sandwiches, use the same knife without wiping it off. The result will be a mixture of condiments and sandwiches that no one wants. Little sex is like using the one knife for multiple sandwiches. But, God can forgive us, wiping the knife clean.

Fire

Light a fire in the fireplace. Discuss how a fire in the right place can be beautiful and romantic, but a fire in the wrong place can be destructive. God designed sex to burn in the marriage bed.

Candy Bar Disaster

Show everyone a candy bar, like a Snickers. Discuss how tempting it is when it is new. Start squeezing the candy bar and passing it around. The candy bar is the same thing it was before, but it is not the same. The more we pass around the gift of sex, the further it gets from what God designed it to be.

MEDIA REINFORCEMENTS

Heaven is a Place on Earth by Belinda Carlisle

God can bring pieces of heaven to earth when we follow his plan for sex.

HEAVEN ON EARTH SEXUAL REVOLUTION

TAKE HOME OBJECTS

Book of Matches

Pass out books of matches to remind people to let God ignite a fire in the marriage bed and to keep the fire burning only in the marriage bed.

OTHER

Personal Reflection

After question 8, give everyone a moment to reflect on their answers and rate how well they are involved in things that will transform their minds. You might discuss strategies for getting better in each area.

LEADER'S GUIDE
SESSION THREE

LEASHED

LEADER'S NOTES

1. **Using your imagination, describe one of your favorite experiences.**

    Tip: Use this as an ice breaker question. Try to get everyone in your group to share at least one memorable experience.

    ⓨ-a *What are songs that are connected to particular moments in your life? For example, a song connected to a Jr. High boyfriend/girlfriend or a road trip.*

    ⓨ-b *What is an example of when you were treated like a number or a product? How did that make you feel?*

2. **Why do you think Jesus took lust so seriously, yet our culture does not?**

    Jesus had a big picture perspective when he talked about lust in Matthew. Knowing that mental adultery is a step toward physical adultery, Jesus wanted to teach us to stay far away from that slippery slope. In contrast, our culture teaches us to lie to ourselves. "It's just a magazine." "It's just a movie." "It's just a song." "It won't affect my mind." We buy into the lies that we're in control, when in reality we are on the edge of the ledge of sexual sin.

    ⓨ-c *What are other examples of rules or boundaries that let us experience more freedom? For example, laws may restrict some of our freedoms but they also protect us from others taking our freedom.*

3. **How could doing things God's way give you a new perspective on other areas of your life?**

    When we trust God in one area and experience his faithfulness, it will encourage us to trust God in other areas. As we experience God's wisdom in one area, it will make us curious about trusting God in another area.

129

LEASHED SEXUAL REVOLUTION

Y-d *What are some things you could do to overcome just seeing a person as a product and see them as fully human instead?*

4. How could being caught in lust lead to legitimate, lifelong pain?

Allowing explicit images and thoughts to occupy space in your brain pushes Godly things out. Without God and righteous things on your mind, your life can quickly spin out of control. Have your group consider the snowball effect of lust leading to infidelity, infidelity leading to divorce, and divorce leading to a destroyed family.

5. What are the dangers of becoming someone who lusts more and more? What can you do to stop those dangers from becoming realities in your life?

The dangers range from personal consequences like guilt and shame to consequences that affect others like broken relationships and broken trust. If we want to avoid these consequences, we have to identify lust as a serious sin. Then, we must seek God's plan for overcoming sin so we can live in freedom. That means focusing on God instead of on lust and asking God for his strength to overcome our temptations. We also need to guard our thoughts and find people to encourage us to make wise decisions.

Y-e *If students identify that they are struggling with lust, encourage them to spend part of their time confessing their sin and asking God for the strength to repent.*

Y-f *When we sin, there will be conviction. How can you tell the difference between conviction that is from God and guilt that is from Satan?*

Y-g *Go to a site like Ebay and look for odd things that are for sale. Find how much someone is willing to pay for those things that others might consider worthless. Whatever someone will pay is what those objects are worth.*

6. Using 1 Peter 1:18-19 and Romans 5:8, what could you say to a friend who is struggling with being leashed to the little bed of lust?

Little bed sex devalues us. God has shown us that despite our disobedience, he values us. Because God values us so much, he desires us to choose his big bed of sex. It does not matter how long we have stayed in the little bed, God can free us and give us the benefits of his wisdom and love in our sex.

Y-h *John 8:44*

7. How have you experienced freedom from sharing a secret with someone you trusted?

Sharing our secrets can strengthen the bonds we have with others, and it can open us up to get Godly advice and guidance from Christ-followers. It can also be a first step toward confessing our sins to God and getting on his path for our lives.

SEXUAL REVOLUTION `LEASHED`

> ⓨ-i *Spend time individually developing a plan for who you could share your secrets with, what you need to share and when you will share those secrets.*

8. How has applying God's principles in the past been a light to your life?
Tip: Challenge your group to think of ways they've applied God's principles with their sexuality as well as in other areas of their lives such as their family, finances, and friendships.

CREATIVE NOTES

ICEBREAKERS

Imaginary Friend

Find out who had imaginary friends when they were younger and ask them to describe them.

BRIDGE – The imagination can be powerful. God desires for our imagination to be used in ways that honor him.

Hobbies

What hobbies are you involved in? How do those hobbies affect your life? For example, golfers spend money on clubs, clothing and tee times. They talk about it when they are not playing. They watch golf on TV, play golfing video games, visit golf websites.

BRIDGE – Lust can become a hobby if we are not careful. It can begin to affect other areas of our lives is we do not give God control.

Different Definitions

Try to guess how the following groups would define lust: guys in a locker room, soccer moms, junior high students, college students, a preacher, and someone in the adult industry. Discuss what you think influences their definition.

BRIDGE – God designed us to respond to visual stimuli. He wants us to put that response under his control so he can fulfill it.

Puzzling Perspective

Get a simple children's puzzle and strong prescription glasses. Have a contest trying to put the puzzle together while wearing the glasses.

BRIDGE – Lust can give us the wrong perspective and cause confusion. God wants to bring clarity to our lives by giving us his perspective on sex.

LEASHED SEXUAL REVOLUTION

HANDS-ON ACTIVITES

Price is Right

Set out common products that you could easily find in a grocery store. Ask each person to write down what they think is the price of each object. Compare answers with the actual cost to see who got the most right.

BRIDGE – If you have ever wondered what you are worth, God demonstrated that you are worth the precious blood of his son Jesus.

Stronger Senses

Look at an object like an apple and describe it based strictly on what you see. Then, use all your other senses except sight to describe the object. Smell it, feel it, taste it, etc. Compare the descriptions and choose which one is a better description.

BRIDGE – Lust only describes a person on one level. God wants us to see the whole person for more than just the way they look.

Secret Sharing Plan

God wants us to confess our sins to each other. Sometimes that means sharing secret parts of our lives. When we take this chance, God will give us freedom. Spend time individually developing a plan to share a secret sin with someone you trust. Write down who you will talk with, when you will contact them, and where you will meet to talk.

BRIDGE – God wants to give us freedom through confessing our sins to each other.

VISUAL REINFORCEMENTS

Owner's Manuals

Place owner's manuals in the middle of your small group. Describe how God has given us the owner's manual for our sexuality through the Bible.

Dog Bowl

Place a dog bowl with food in the middle of the group. God wants us to remember we are humans, not hounds. Lust reduces us to animals.

SEXUAL REVOLUTION LEASHED

TAKE HOME OBJECTS

Take Home Cards

Make cards with the following verses written on them about who we are in God and how he sees us: John 3:16; Romans 5:8; Romans 8:1, 16-17; 2 Corinthians 5:17.

OTHER

Filters

Most of us have filters on our computers to protect us from downloading viruses or spam. God wants us to have a filter on what we see and hear to protect us from unhealthy influenences.

Following Directions

How many of you open things and ignore the directions? When has following the directions enhanced your enjoyment of a product? It is good to know if we have a natural tendency to ignore directions because it can cause us to ignore God's directions.

Naked Nightmare

Have you ever had the dream that you went to school naked? The thought of exposing ourselves in that way is scary, but many will expose themselves through sex in relationships with no real commitment.

LEADER'S GUIDE
SESSION FOUR

DO YOUR THING

LEADER'S NOTES

1. **How old were you when your parents talked with you about sex? What do you remember from those conversations?**

    Tip: Parents talking with their children about sex has become content for TV sitcoms and movies. Many parents struggle to communicate out of awkwardness or embarrassment. You will get some of those awkward stories. If anyone has a story of when the conversation was comfortable, ask them what contributed to that positive experience.

    (Y)-a *Most of your students do not have any children, but they can still be influential. The decisions they make can influence their friends and teach them about God's plan for sex. Also, their parents might not do a good job modeling for them how to talk to their children about sex, so they need to learn somewhere. Today can be a great opportunity.*

    (Y)-b *What could your parents do to create an environment where you would want to learn form them about sex? What could you do to encourage that kind of environment?*

    (Y)-c *In general, how can you impress God's commands on your heart?*

2. **How could you apply Deuteronomy 6:6-9 to teaching your children about God's plan for sex?**

    Teaching your children about sex is not just a one time talk. It should be something that happens on a continuous basis. Also, talks about sex should be more than just the specifics of intercourse. There should be discussions about the spiritual, emotional and other sides of sex. Part of sex education being more than just a one-time talk is talking as images of little sex are encountered. Use those as opportunities to discuss God's plan for big sex.

135

DO YOUR THING SEXUAL REVOLUTION

3. **Growing up, where did you get most of your information about sex and how accurate was the information you got?**

    Tip: Make a list of valuable places where you got your information and places that gave you information that was more damaging than good. Then, use that as a way to discuss how your children get their information about sex. You should be able to come up with good sources for getting their information as well as sources you want to protect them from.

    (Y)-d *If your parents are not a good source for your information about sex, where could you get good information about God's plan for big sex?*

4. **What were positive things your parents did to teach you about sex? Or, what have you heard of other parents doing to teach their children about sex?**

    Sex needs to be more than a "Don't do it" talk. Sex is a good gift from God that should be taught in a positive way. Instead of focusing on the dangers of little sex, the focus should be on the greatness of God's plan for sex. You need to warn your children about the dangers of little sex, but that does not have to be the focus. Also, being honest about little and big sex is valuable. Little sex has some attractiveness in the short run, but the damage done in the long run is not worth the immediate satisfaction. By painting an honest picture of sex you prepare your children for what they will encounter and equip them to make wise decisions.

    (Y)-e *If you were a parent, what would you do to teach your children about sex?*

5. **What are things you think are important to creating an environment to teach children about sex?**

    Modeling the right decisions about sex is an important place to start. If a parent tries to teach their children that sex is a gift for marriage then goes around sharing that gift outside of marriage, the message will be mixed. Also, seek to create an open relationship where children can ask their parents honest questions and get honest answers. On top of that, demonstrating that God's principles can be trusted in other areas makes God's principles for sex easier to trust.

    (Y)-f *If you found out your parents had made bad decisions, how would that affect your opinion of them? What could they do to make that discovery something positive?*

    (Y)-g *Are the decisions you are making today, something you will want your children to find out about, or your spouse to find out about? Would you want to find out your spouse made the same decisions you made?*

6. **What are some practical ways you could insulate your children without isolating them?**

    If you want to insulate them, you have to be involved in their lives. You must know who and what is influencing them. This takes spending time with them and their friends.

SEXUAL REVOLUTION DO YOUR THING

This also takes being aware of what they are doing when you are not around.

Once you know what is influencing them, you can set up safer environments for them. You could make your home a place where everyone is invited to hang out. Simple things like having food for them and the willingness to open your home creates this type of opportunity.

Ⓨ-h *How have you fought your parents' insulation and why did you fight them?*

7. **How well did your parents monitor you growing up? What did they do that was good and what do you wish they would have done?**

   Tip: Listen for common themes in the answers that were positive and negative to develop general guidelines for them in monitoring their children.

Ⓨ-i *If you have a younger brother or sister, you have a responsibility to set a good example for them. If you are setting an example that will encourage them to try out little sex, you will be accountable to God.*

CREATIVE NOTES

ICEBREAKERS

Guess Who

Have each lady put on lipstick and kiss a poster board. Others members have to guess whose kiss is whose. Then, talk about what influenced your understanding of kissing.

BRIDGE – Hopefully no one was embarrassed like Ed when they learned to kiss.

Where and When?

Ask where and when did you first hear about sex?

BRIDGE – Sometimes the information we received about sex was accurate and sometimes it was not. As parents, God wants us to teach our kids his way before they are influenced by other perspectives.

Where Do Babies Come From?

Brainstorm a list of answers parents have given for where babies come from. For example: the stork, cabbage patch, etc.

DO YOUR THING SEXUAL REVOLUTION

BRIDGE – There are lots of answers for where babies come from, but God wants our children to know the truth. That means more than just teaching them the anatomical part of sex. God wants them to know his design for sex.

HANDS-ON ACTIVITIES

Remodel

Rewrite Deuteronomy 6:6-9 with modern examples.

BRIDGE – God wants us to live out this verse in our lives.

Kid Questions

Kids have a way of asking the most difficult questions. They want honest answers that can be easily understood. What are some of the questions you have heard your kids or others ask about sex?

BRIDGE – God has given us the responsibility to educate our children about sex. We need to know God's plan for sex so we can offer honest and clear answers when our children ask.

Color Copy

Show the group a colorful picture of something like a flower. Give each person one crayon and tell them to draw the same picture. Compare the pictures to determine whose one color version was the best.

BRIDGE – Explaining sex with just one conversation is like reproducing the colorful picture with only one color. Our children need to hear about sex through many different conversations to paint a true picture of what God wants.

VISUAL REINFORCEMENTS

Best Beach

Show a picture of the beach at Galveston or South Padre Island and a picture of the beach in the Bahamas or Hawaii. South Padre Island and Galveston look like a great if you have never seen the Bahamas or Hawaii. Little sex looks good but is nothing compared to God's plan for sex.

SEXUAL REVOLUTION DO YOUR THING

Blindfold or Sunglasses

Have a blindfold to represent isolation and sunglasses to represent insulation. The leaders can each wear one to emphasize the difference. God wants us to insulate our children to protect them, but not isolate them and blind them from what is happening around them.

MEDIA REINFORCEMENTS

Watching You by Rodney Atkins

The song is a reminder to parents of how children imitate their parents.

I Want to be Just like You by Phillips, Craig and Dean

The father in the song knows his son will imitate him so the father is trying to imitate God.

TAKE HOME OBJECTS

Little Reflections

Pass out mirrors to remind everyone that their children will be a reflection of them.

Ostrich Head

Give each member some sand in a small container to remind them not to stick their head in the sand when it comes to talking with their kids about sex (You could also pass out blindfolds or sleeping masks using the same point).

OTHER

Monitor

Pose the question, "What areas of your child's life do you think are the most important to monitor and how should you do it?"

LEADER'S GUIDE
SESSION FIVE

MESSED UP

LEADER'S NOTES

1. **What have you learned from this study that has impacted you the most?**

2. **Spend a moment silently thinking about what influences your thoughts on sex. Consider the people you hang around and the relationships you are in. What course are you setting for sexual intercourse?**

    Tip: Once you have given them a chance to privately think about the influences, let them share what they learned. Ask if they are content with the course they are setting or if they identified changes they needed to make. Don't push for specifics and guard your group from sharing too much information that they may regret later.

3. **How would you explain to a friend who was thinking about jumping in the little bed for little sex that there is no such thing as "just sex"?**

    God created us as spiritual beings and whether we admit it or not, sex is a spiritual act. God designed it to unite two people in more than just a physical sense. Sex outside of God's plan neglects the emotional and spiritual connection of sex. The physical act of sex affects us spiritually and emotionally by either wounding us or making us callous. Only sex in marriage can lead to the full physical, emotional and spiritual connection God designed.

    Ⓨ-a Saying it is "just sex" is like saying "there is just a little poison in that cookie" or "I am going to just cut a little of your finger off." That is not possible. The consequences are too severe for both of those things and so are the consequences for little sex. It is too significant to be "just sex."

141

MESSED UP SEXUAL REVOLUTION

4. What are some practical things you could do to develop the nonsexual elements of your relationship?

The date night is a great way to incorporate several of the nonsexual elements. You have the opportunity to make romantic plans that engage your spouse (or date) in ways that take into consideration what they consider romantic. On the date, you have the opportunity for conversation. Practice sharing more than surface level information. Sharing dreams and insecurities can create at least understanding if not intimacy.

(Y)-b *What are some nonsexual things you could do to show your boyfriend or girlfriend that you care?*

(Y)-c *Many of the issues we struggle with are the same as they were years ago. Share some of the major issues in your high school that are the same as the issues students deal with today.*

5. How could you distance yourself from sexual immorality without alienating yourself from people who need to know God loves them?

Set clear boundaries for yourself. Know places you will not go or conversations you will not have. Excuse yourself when you are about to cross a boundary with respect for the other person. You can also invite others to join your plans in an attempt to positively influence them.

6. What do you think are some good guidelines for what we should wear and not wear?

Clothing decisions should be made based on more than just your perspective. Try to think about the opposite sex's perspective on what you are wearing. What will their attention be drawn to and what does that communicate about you? On top of that, you must consider how your clothing will impact people's perspective on God. It might be good to consider if you could comfortably share your faith in what you are about to put on.

(Y)-d *For girls groups, bring magazines that show images of fashion and have them look at the different examples. Ask them to look at those pictures how they think guys might look at them and consider whether or not those fashion choices are appropriate.*

7. How can obedience in the area of sex affect your relationship with God?

Sin abuses and confuses in every area of our lives. When we choose to live apart from God's plan, we are going to experience the mess that creates. When we choose to live according to God's plan, we can experience the blessings that come with that.

8. What are some decisions you can make to help you stay committed to purity?

One of the biggest decisions is to establish clear boundaries before you are tempted. When you wait until you are tempted, you will make decisions you regret. Study God's

SEXUAL REVOLUTION `MESSED UP`

Word to establish your boundaries. Then, have a core group of friends that support you and encourage you to keep those biblical boundaries.

Ⓨ-e *Encourage each student to write down decisions they need to make to stay pure. Then, have them identify someone they could choose to help keep them stay accountable.*

The accountability partner can be a great help, but we are only as accountable as we want to be. If we don't want to be helped out through accountability, we can easily lie or make excuses to the people there to help us. So, before we ask someone to help us, we need to make sure that is something we really want.

CREATIVE NOTES

ICEBREAKERS

Setting a Course

Pass out paper and a pen to everyone. Let them write down the people and events that influenced their course of understanding sex. Have them write down things in their life right now that are influencing their future course for sex. Have them think about where they will be in a few years if they keep the same course.

BRIDGE – God wants us to recognize we are all setting a course for sexual intercourse.

It's About the Non-Sexual Stuff

Divide up into two groups – men and women. Let the men brainstorm the non-sexual stuff they think is important to women and let the women brainstorm the non-sexual stuff they think is important to men. Let them share their answers with each other and see how well they knew the opposite sex.

BRIDGE – God wants to develop the non-sexual stuff before we get married and cultivate the non-sexual stuff once we are married so we can have the great sex he designed.

MESSED UP SEXUAL REVOLUTION

HANDS-ON ACTIVITIES

Wiped Clean

Bring a chalkboard or dry erase board and have each person sign their name on the board. When you talk about God's forgiveness, erase the names off the board to show how God can forgive decisions of our past.

BRIDGE — God always forgives our sin when we ask.

Trinity Cookies

Have members try to eat just the chocolate chips out of a chocolate chip cookie without destroying the cookie.

BRIDGE — Little sex tries to pick out pieces of sex, but it destroys the whole thing. God understands sex involves multiple areas of our lives and when we try to just pick out certain areas, we destroy what God designed.

VISUAL REINFORCEMENTS

OxyClean

Place a dirty rag in OxyClean to demonstrate God's forgiveness. God can make us pure no matter what we have done.

I Can't See!

Pass around glasses that are scratched and smudged. We cannot see the greatness of God's plan for sex when we our perspective is scratched and smudged with a little view of sex.

Gown, Anyone?

Get a hospital gown and ask people if they can remember how it felt to wear a hospital gown? Most are uncomfortable because of over exposure. Little sex exposes us in ways God never intended us to be exposed.

Set Apart

On one plate have a bunch of broken cookies. On another plate, have whole ones. God wants us to be set apart and whole; not broken.

Which Way Is North?

Use a compass to illustrate God points us in the right direction. Place a large magnet

SEXUAL REVOLUTION `MESSED UP`

next to the compass (it will not give an accurate read anymore). Getting involved in little sex pushes us off the direction God has chosen for us and leads us into confusion.

TAKE HOME OBJECTS

Eraser

God cleans up our past.

Great Sex Recipe Card

Pass out recipe cards for great sex: marriage, romance, intimacy, conversation, and environment.

Now and Later

Pass out the candy "Now and Later" as a reminder that following God's plan will lead to satisfaction now and later.

Outrageous, Contagious Joy

Five Big Questions to Help You Discover One Great Life

What if there was more to life than you ever thought possible? Something beyond your wildest dreams? What if your days and weeks consisted of more than just waiting for the next payday, or the next acquisition, or the next boyfriend/girlfriend, or the next fun fix, or the next happy feeling, or the next whatever? What if you could have a bigger, more meaningful life right now?

Ed Young shares five life-altering questions and eye-opening insights that will steer you to what he calls *Outrageous, Contagious Joy*. In this inspiring, straightforward guide, he shows you the way to improve your life and find your divine purpose. It all begins with five simple yet profound questions:

- Does God want you to be happy?
- Where are you headed?
- Who are you running with?
- Why are you here?
- What are you working for?

Created to help you think about where you are and where you are going, this remarkable book will give you very specific and practical steps that will revolutionize the way you think of —and carry out—your life, and lead you to *Outrageous, Contagious Joy*.

Buy your copy today!

Available on CreativePastors.com or anywhere good books are sold.

Berkley hardcover, 352 pages

CHECK OUT THESE OTHER STUDIES BY ED YOUNG AVAILABLE ON CREATIVEPASTORS.COM:

A Bout With Doubt
Responding To Global Turmoil And Personal Doubt

Doubt is not a cosmic crime or a blockade to your spiritual growth. When we take our bouts with doubt to God, he will allow them to strengthen our faith and draw us closer to him. This study is designed to teach us the right response to doubt.

Retro
Getting Back To The Basics

Juggling life's priorities can easily become complicated and complex. In this series, Ed Young takes a closer look at the essentials for a strong Christian life, including building the right friendships, involvement in the local church, developing biblical priorities and taking time to rest.

Forgiveness - The Real F-Word
Unleashing The Power Of Forgiveness

Forgiveness feels great—as long as we are the beneficiaries. We like being forgiven, but it's not very fun when you have to ask for forgiveness. Through this study, we will discover God's powerful truths about this highly-charged subject of forgiveness.

Snapshots of the Savior
Jesus—Up Close And Personal

So often when we think of Jesus' life, our photo album is limited and sketchy. In this powerful study of talks, Ed Young shares vivid images from the Bible to help provide a broader, panoramic view of Christ's mission and ministry.

The Creative Marriage
The Art Of Keeping Your Love Alive

Disposable relationships and throw-away marriages permeate our culture. When the dream fades and the realities of life set in, many just throw in the towel. In this six-week study, Ed speaks openly and honestly about the hard work involved in a creative marriage and the lasting rewards of doing it God's way.

In The Zone
How To Live In The Sweet Spot Of Success

Do you want to live a life in marked contrast to those around you? In this study, Ed Young shares powerful biblical principles about what it means to live a life blessed by God—to live *in the zone*.

The Table
Casting The Vision For The Local Church

The foundational series for small groups by Ed Young uniquely relates different aspects of eating a special meal to our purpose as Christ followers. As we focus on serving others, it reminds us in a powerful way that there's always room at the table.

Mission Possible
Everyday Leadership Principles For Everyday People

With an impossible mission before him, Nehemiah allowed God to develop him as a leader and to give him the skills and character necessary to carry out his mission successfully. This study uncovers the timeless leadership principles found in this Old Testament power struggle between conniving political leaders and a persevering construction mogul.

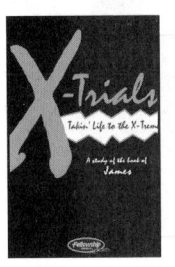

X-Trials – Takin' Life to the X-Treme
An Extreme Study In The Book Of James

In this book, *X-Trials*, Ed Young leads you through a verse-by-verse look at one of the most challenging and controversial books of the Bible, the book of James. Living life as a Christ-follower in today's world requires extreme faith!

Character Tour
A Biblical Tour Of Some Great Characters With Great Character

Certain character qualities stand out in notable characters throughout the Bible. In this creative series, Ed Young uses those great biblical role models to help us crack the character code and become people who live out godly character from the inside out.

Virtuous Reality
The Relationships Of David

People in your life can pull you up or drag you down. Join this journey into the life of David as we discover how this "man after God's own heart" lived out the daily reality of his relationships. By uncovering the good and bad in your relationships, Ed Young will help you discover how to honor God regardless of who crosses your path.

Ignite
Refining And Purifying Your Faith

Fire, it is a source of destruction and a source of life. It incinerates and destroys. But it also refines and purifies. In the Bible, God used fire and other trials to turn up the heat and reveal His power through the lives of people. Ed Young explores these trials from Scripture to help fan the flames of our own faith today.

Tri-GOD
Understanding The Trinity
Three in One, One in Three. The Trinity. God in three persons—Father, Son, and Holy Spirit—is one of the most misunderstood doctrines in the Christian church. Yet Ed Young teaches in this exciting new series that our awareness of God's triune nature is pivotal to growing with Him.

First and 10
The Whats, Whys And Hows Of The Ten Commandments
Where do we find our moral foundation in this game of life? In a world of ever-changing culture, circumstances, and philosophies it all goes back to the big ten. Ed Young will take you on a thought-provoking, soul-searching look at the Ten Commandments.

Wired for Worship
Make Worship A Part Of Your Every Day Life
There is great debate and misconception surrounding "worship." One thing holds true, as human beings we are wired for worship. Whether it is career and finances or relationships and family, we instinctively worship something. Join Ed Young as he dives in to discover what it means to truly worship God in your life.

Praying for Keeps
A Guide To Prayer
Imagine how awesome it would be to sit down and have a face-to-face conversation with God! In the small group study, you will learn how you can effectively and naturally communicate with God. Ed Young will walk you through the biblical principles that will guide you into a more intimate and rewarding life of prayer.

Fatal Distractions
Avoid The Downward Spiral Of Sin
In this in-depth study, Pastor Ed Young makes a frontal assault on the seven deadly sins that threaten to destroy our lives.

RPMs - Recognizing Potential Mates
Supercharge Your Dating Life
Whether you're a single adult, a student, or a parent, this creatively driven study will provide foundational principles on how to date and select a mate God's way. We're going to cruise past the cultural myths and embark on a supercharged ride to the ultimate relational destination.